# WHO HELPS THE HELPER?

# WHO HELPS THE HELPER?

*Proven Stress Management Techniques
for Law Enforcement Officers*

## DEBORAH C. MOORE

*Ph.D., LMFT, Lieutenant, (NYPD), (ret).*

**Who Helps the Helper?**

© 2013 by Deborah C. Moore

Maltese Publishing

ISBN: 978-0-9884999-0-4

Library of Congress Control Number: 2012919587

Author Website: DrDebiMoore.org

Cover Photo: ShutterStock
Cover Design and Interior Layout: AuthorSupport.com

# *Dedication*

This book is dedicated to all the men and women who risk their lives and emotional well-being to ensure our communities are safe. The job you do is dangerous, yet essential, and we, as a society, would suffer without your dedication, patience and bravery. More importantly, this book is dedicated to my little sister, Police Officer Charlene D. Moore, who had the courage to follow in her big sister's footsteps.

# *Acknowledgements*

My thanks go out first and foremost to my parents, Evelyn and Charles, for their love and unstinting support for me over the years. I can never truly repay the debt I owe them, but I can note it here. I would also like to thank the many fine law enforcement professionals of the New York City Police Department who supported and encouraged me during the course of a long and rewarding career. Finally, my gratitude goes to all of you who have helped make this book possible.

# Contents

**PART III** *Appendices*

# PART I

# "You'd Like Being
An Officer"

# CHAPTER ONE

# *In The City*

*"The only person you are destined to become*
*is the person you decide to be."*
—RALPH WALDO EMERSON

N ot every minority kid in an urban area grows up with positive feelings about the city's police department. Not every Black American in the inner city remembers only friendships with the officers who comprise that department. But that's the way it was for me.

Police officers in New York City make a point of community policing. That means that people in the community who have questions can usually get to know officers

one-on-one pretty easily, because they *want* you to get
to know them as people, as part of the community. The
goal is always to be seen more as trusted arbitratrors and
problem-solvers than as members of some kind of an
occupying force. Some of those officers left an indelible
impression on me as I was growing up.

One of them was a striking woman with piercing eyes
and an immaculately pressed uniform who came to visit
our class while I was in eleventh grade. I'll call her Detective Reynolds. She was huge – not in weight but in strength
and brawn. She was well over six feet tall and she carried
herself with the kind of poise and confidence and profes-
sionalism that instantly commanded the attention of our
(usually very talkative) class. I had never seen or heard anyone like her. The whole idea of a black woman like Detective Reynolds walking into a room and calming it down,
simply with her presence, was deeply appealing to me.

Detective Reynolds came back week after week —
she was part of an anti-drug program we had back then
in the inner cities, and which is still quite active, known
as DARE. (It stands for Drug Abuse Resistance Education.) Detective Reynolds was there to talk to us, but she
was also there to listen. She wanted to hear our stories,

and, wherever she could, she wanted to share insights from her own past that would make it easier for us to do the right thing and stay out of trouble.

We all looked forward to her visits, as I remember it, and not just because it meant a break from our regular classwork. Officer Reynolds was really there to give us a reality check: about life as a young adult in New York City, about the kinds of choices we would all be facing once we got out of high school, and about what the right (and wrong) choices looked like and felt like. Basically, she was talking to us about how to take a stand for ourselves, how to keep us from becoming statistics in the big ongoing national news story we saw every night on TV: the story about drugs and violence in the streets. She was there to help us.

Officer Reynolds and I became friends. I always found a reason to stick around after her presentation and talk to her about what she did, and she always had amazing stories to tell. One day, while we were talking, I heard myself say, "You know, I wouldn't mind doing what you do."

She smiled a big smile. And looking back now, I realize that that smile of hers marked one of the big moments in my life, a moment when my whole life changed.

"You'd like being an officer."

Could Detective Reynolds have been right when she told me that? I certainly didn't know at the time, but I was willing to find out.

My schoolroom encounter with Detective Reynolds's unique style of "community policing" had set a whole new destiny in motion for me. The experience of hearing a powerful black woman speak with authority, week in and week out, about the dos and don'ts of society, about how to stay out of trouble, about what could get you killed, right here in Queens, *because she genuinely cared about us* — that was something new. The experience had not only gotten my attention, but it had also awakened a part of me that proved to be a very powerful force in my adult life. I'll try to explain that force briefly now, although I have to say I'm using words and experiences to describe it that I didn't have back then.

> *"Our lives were just beginning, our favorite*
> *moment was right now, our favorite*
> *songs were unwritten."*
> —Rob Sheffield

After I had those sessions with Detective Reynolds, I realized there was something about her discussions with us that kept on drawing me toward the possibility of being a police officer. I just kept thinking about her job, and about how much that job really encompassed. Before she showed up in our classroom, I had never even considered that police officers could do things like visit schools ... because before she arrived, I tended to think of police officers simply as authority figures. They were the ones who put other people under arrest, the ones who were there to enforce the law, period. Now, after talking to her, I understood that while doing those things was obviously part of her prime duty, there was another part of her job that was also extremely important: interacting with people one-on-one and helping them to resolve their issues in a positive, constructive way ... before those issues turned into big problems.

This was my first exposure to the idea that a police officer was someone who was there to interact with you, someone who could talk to you and help you to work something out — not as a member of some kind of occupying force, but as a friend and ally who was there to help you find a good outcome. I realize now that Detective Reynolds had introduced me to something very important: the human side of police work.

The more I thought about the personal connections she made with those of us in the classroom, the more intrigued I became with something about what she was doing, something that I now realize was at the heart of her profession: her desire to connect with people and help them, in much the same way a counselor, therapist, doctor, pastor, or rabbi would help someone.

That fascinated me. (Looking back, I realize now how that youthful fascination eventually matured, strengthened, and led me to the later phase of my career, as a counselor who specializes in peer work with police officers.)

\*　　\*　　\*

I took the test. I studied hard to make sure that I got a good score, and I felt that I had done well.

# CHAPTER TWO

# At The Academy

*Live as if you were to die tomorrow.*
*Learn as if you were to live forever.*

—Mahatma Gandhi

I t wasn't until a couple of years later that I was actually called to join the police force. (My application process was delayed, which I later learned was not all that uncommon an occurrence.) At that point I decided I wanted to be, not a police officer, but a therapist. However, I knew I still had a long way to go. There were a lot of things I hadn't quite settled about my career path, yet I still knew I had a passion to help people. I knew

I wanted to become some kind of therapist or counselor someday. Beyond that I hadn't yet filled in many of the blanks. I had just finished my Associate's Degree in Mental Health ... when the Police Department finally called me. The call came as a big surprise because I had assumed that the long silence after my exam meant that I hadn't been selected.

My degree, it turned out, had helped to separate me from the pack. At that time it was very rare for someone who had a college degree of any kind to join the force. During the early 1990s, when I joined the police force, not only did most new police officers not have a college degree, but a fair number did not even have high school diplomas. You didn't need to have finished high school to become a police officer in New York City back then. A GED and good test score was sufficient! Times have certainly changed. You need at least a few years of college now to become a police officer in the Big Apple.

At any rate, at the time I got that call from the department, I was certainly not expecting to become an officer any more. I had turned the page and moved on to what I thought was my next chapter. Before that phone rang, all I had known for sure about what I wanted to do next was that it was time to for me to go on to get a bachelor's degree. Once I got the call from the department, though, I didn't have to think very long about what I was going to do next. I didn't have to talk to anyone about it; I didn't have to sleep on it. Something deep inside told me: "This is the right next move."

I listened to that little voice. I said to myself, "You know what? I'll join the police force. That will help supplement my income and help me pay my tuition." But I need to do some full disclosure here: as much of an impact as Detective Reynolds had on my early life, at this point my long-term career goal was *not* to work for the police department. That was definitely not what kept me up at night. Thinking about what I could do with my life, is what gave me sleepless nights. My goal was to support myself while I worked toward my next degree. I told myself that I would give the NYPD five years then move on and get a job somewhere else. In reality, it turned out a lot differently. My five-year plan eventually turned into a law enforcement career of a little over twenty years!

\*     \*     \*

To become an officer, I had to make it through six months of intensive training at the Police Academy. The Police Academy was located in Manhattan—roughly a twenty-minute commute from where I lived. The building was old, bleak and harsh-looking, inside and out. We saluted the American flag each time we entered the building. And each time we entered, there were police officers at the front door waiting to poke fun at the new police recruits.

There were so many thoughts tumbling through my mind on the first day. What was going to happen? Was I ready for this? Could I learn what was necessary to protect people in dangerous situations? Could I learn what was necessary to protect *myself, and others?* For me, that last one was a major question because I'm not a big person. Most people describe me as petite or (to use the phrase I preferred) *compact.*

It was a challenging environment, which was exactly what it was supposed to be: challenging and intimidating. This experience is difficult, and it is meant to separate the strong from the weak, meant to get some people to quit. This was trial by fire. Yes, the Academy is about the tactical elements of the job as well as the fundamentals: policing, police science, and also social science skills. And yes, there were plenty of physical challenges to overcome. But the core experience, the core challenge, the core test, was really psychological. Policing is thought of as being mostly physical and tactical, but there were psychological issues to confront as well. For six months the Academy constantly poses a tough question: Are you ready—not just physically, not just academically but as a matter of personal identity—to step up and become a police officer in New York City?

Looking back, I think there were challenges on a number of sides, and I think I did well in meeting them. But the early days were difficult.

*Change is the end result of all true learning.*
—LEO BUSCAGLIA

As a *compact* woman, I encountered my share of stereotypes and prejudice from other officers and trainees. Some of it was spoken out loud, a lot of it was gestures and glances, but most of it was designed to get me to leave the Academy. I think a lot of people still felt, at that point, that women probably should not be police officers. Since then, viewpoints have changed significantly. But, back then, this was a major obstacle. A lot of people thought that we just plain didn't belong in the Academy.

I'd hear people say things like, "It's a female. She's not going to be able to hack it." Or: "She won't be able to do the pushups." Or: "She won't be able to do the required number of sit-ups." There was a lot of that, and I'm sure there was a lot said that I didn't hear. Of course, they weren't really talking about pushups and sit-ups. The implication was, "She's not going to be able to handle herself in a dangerous situation, or protect a partner, or protect a civilian." I made a mental note, early on, that I would have to hit all the physical targets set for me if I expected to earn the respect of my peers.

That was the reason that I never, ever dropped out of runs. That was always a major topic of discussion: which woman had dropped out of the run that day. You had to run a mile and a half in a certain amount of time, and if you bailed out, people talked about you. I always beat the time I was supposed to beat. The women who dropped out of the mile-and-a-half runs paid a price for it in terms of the things other people in training said about them.

So I did find that I had to continuously prove myself, more so than my male counterparts did ... and I even had to prove myself to the females that were slightly bigger than me. But I found that I was okay with that. Something within me responded well to the challenge of proving my ability, both as a "petite" female and as a member of a minority group. (Remember, at this point in the NYPD's history, there weren't as many minorities being hired as there are now because the outreach to that community had really only just begun.)

I set my sights on the goal of showing that I could handle anything and everything that the Academy chose to throw my way. I decided early on that the short-term pain of finishing any given task and hitting the target was going to be a lot less than the long-term pain of giving up. This was an important distinction, because the reputation you build up for yourself in the Academy is very, very important in your later career in policing. Some things really do follow you throughout your life and career; first impressions really do count. So doing the pushups, the sit-ups, and making the time you were supposed to make in the run, these were all very important formative stages, both in terms of your internal development and in terms of your reputation. Whatever happens during those six months of training will tend to follow you throughout your career. I certainly saw that among a lot of my counterparts at the Academy.

Pushups I could handle. Sit-ups I could handle. Running I could handle. The most difficult physical challenge I faced, though, involved weight training. As you know by now, I am not a big lady. I was five foot five and about a hundred and twenty pounds. And one of the requirements at the Academy was that you had to be able to bench press one-half of your body weight—that one seemed pretty intense, even for someone as *compact* as I.

For anyone who is not familiar with weight training, the bench press requires the person performing the exercise to lower a weight to the level of the chest then push it back up until his or her arms are straight again. This is an exercise for the development of a wide range of muscle groups, and the barbell bench press—which is what I was told at the Academy I had to do—is used extensively in weight training to develop chest and arm strength. It's great for that. But it's not easy. I had never bench-pressed anything before, much less half of my body weight.

Lowering sixty pounds of barbells to my chest then raising my arms to bring the weights back up was a major, major challenge for me. Initially, I couldn't see how I would ever be able to do it. I tried, and at first I could not even lift the bar. After a few weeks of training, the barbells came down all right, but they didn't go back up.

It quickly became apparent that I was going to have to build up my muscle strength progressively if I was ever going to be able to lift that much. My instructor was a burly, experienced guy I'll call Officer Walters, who did a very good impression of someone who doubted my ability to meet the standard. Thinking about it now, I realize he wouldn't have invested so much time, effort, and energy badgering me about how I couldn't possibly hit the goal if he didn't think I had some kind of potential as an officer. So he was certainly a mentor of sorts. However, while I was sweating on the bench, trying to work up the arm strength necessary to control steadily larger weights, it didn't always feel like he was on my side.

Officer Walters would say things like, "Moore, you're wasting your time. You're so tiny; you're never going to be able to lift this. You might as well bail out of the Academy now."

And, "Moore, do you realize I can lift two of you with one arm? And you can't lift half of yourself using two?"

And another favorite, "Moore, do you think you're fooling anybody? You're just too small to be an officer. You know it. I know it. And everyone else knows it, too."

He didn't sound like he was helping me, and it certainly didn't feel like he was helping me, but the truth is, he was. He knew how important it was to me to show everyone that I could do this. And so he played to it.

When I finally bench-pressed the sixty pounds, I felt like I had conquered the world. It was as though I had moved a mountain. I knew for sure now that I was going to be able to gain the respect of my male counterparts. And that's what happened. Once I had proved to them, yes, I was just as strong, just as confident, just as adept, just as committed, just as well-trained tactically as anyone else in the Academy, the road became a lot smoother. I became one of those women on the force who didn't have a whole lot of problems with people disrespecting them. There were moments and incidents every once in a while, sure, but the big question was settled. I knew I belonged in the NYPD, and so did everyone else.

The main thing the training did was to instill a sense of confidence in me. There was no longer any uncertainty about what would happen, or whether I could handle myself in uniform. After that experience with Officer Walters, I had confidence that I really would be able to become a good officer. (And he did, too.)

I was now certain I could go out into the streets of New York City and not only protect myself, but also protect others. For me to be able to come out of training and successfully shoot a firearm at a moving target (note the word *moving*), having never held a firearm of any kind in my entire life, was a major achievement, just as mastering the tactical material and overcoming the physical challenges. All those elements added up to a new sense of ability and purpose in my life, to a certainty that I could successfully finish up the program and move forward to the next phase of my career: patrol duty.

# CHAPTER THREE

# On The Street

*One cannot answer for one's courage when one
has never been in danger.*

—François de La Rochefoucauld

A t the time I got called to join the police department, there was a big push for safe streets, which
meant there was a big push for more "feet on the
street." I was sworn in while David Dinkins, who had
placed great importance on hiring police, was the mayor.
I started on patrol in 1991.

Whenever I went out, I was told I would be working in high-crime areas. I thought, "That's an interesting

way to break in a rookie!" I was put on something called the Tactical Patrol Force, commonly known as TPF. This unit targeted the very highest crime areas in the city (the unit has since been disbanded). I worked throughout New York City in all five boroughs.

Back in the early nineties, crime was rampant in New York City. Robberies, drug use, murders, burglaries—you name it. Everything you didn't want to see the numbers increasing for, were increasing. I still remember the long shifts: from eight at night until four in the morning, working some of the most dangerous streets in the city. Here I was, a twenty-year-old rookie officer, sometimes by myself on patrol, out in some of the toughest areas of Brooklyn, Manhattan, and the Bronx.

Very often, in those early days, I would take a deep breath and wonder to myself, "What in the world am I doing here?" I didn't always have a good answer.

I've often been asked about whether there was a moment when I knew I had made the right decision in joining the force, rather than taking what might have seemed the safer, easier choice of finding another job with which to support myself as I worked toward my Masters. The event that confirmed my choice was one I remember as though it were yesterday.

I was working in Brooklyn, on patrol by myself, in a subway station. At the time, we worked a lot in subway stations in targeted, high-crime areas. That was my assignment: keeping an eye on the subway crowds in a very tough corner of Brooklyn. Don't ask me why it made sense to send a rookie out alone into that kind of environment; I'm just telling you what happened.

I was on duty, watching the people get on and off the train, when I saw three males, probably teens, smoking. Of course there's a "no smoking" law that covers the subway station. So I was thinking, "Well, I can't let them smoke in my train station. I'm here, in full uniform. People in the station are looking at me like, 'What are you going to do?' I've got to do something. "

I realized pretty quickly that I had to figure out a way to get them to put those cigarettes out. I went up to the young men, I stated politely that I was a police officer and asked them to put the cigarette out. They stared back at me. At that moment, I noticed one of the individuals had a gun in his waistband. So, without even thinking, without any hesitation, I physically turned him around.

Now, remember, I'm five foot five, and this gentleman was around six feet tall—and yet it felt completely natural, completely necessary, completely *right* to simply spin him around and retrieve the gun out of his waistband. Yes, I had been trained in such things. But this wasn't practice. It was the real thing. And it had come to me absolutely naturally. Detective Reynolds would have been proud.

I heard people talking and whispering around us. I think everyone was in a state of shock: "Oh, my God, I can't believe she did that." But I did, and now I had to think about what to do with these guys.

I can't tell you how many people have asked me whether I was scared at that moment. The truth is I wasn't. I was too busy to be scared. At the time something like that happens, you're not thinking about the possible consequences because you're on automatic pilot. You're just moving forward to the next thing you need to do. In my case, the next thing I needed to do was call for assistance to help me escort these three individuals back to the precinct. The guys did as I told them. The car showed up. They were taken away.

My first arrest—and it was for unlawful gun possession—a gun collar. That was a big deal. And I had done it on my own. Maybe I *was* supposed to be doing this.

The event made quite a splash with the other officers at the precinct. "Oh my God, you made a gun collar?" "Moore made a gun collar?" "She made a gun collar by herself out there?" For a rookie cop, this experience was a pretty good one. It helped me win some trust and respect from officers who had a great deal more experience than I did. From that point on, people in the Department who heard about what happened were thinking, "She's rocking and rolling out there. She's out working on the streets and getting things accomplished. I wouldn't mind being her partner."

It turned out that patrol duty was exactly the right thing for me at that point in time. I was active. I wrote a lot of summonses and made a lot of arrests in some potentially dangerous situations, including another gun collar just a week later. All from this little tiny rookie. It was pretty cool. And the coolest part of all, the part I couldn't stop thinking about, was that Detective Reynolds had been right: I actually enjoyed this job.

Everything had proceeded without incident. In fact, that particular arrest turned out to be quite a coup for me. It was the first time I was able to apprehend a fairly high-profile person for unlawful gun possession. He was a big guy—in more ways than one. It turned out that the man I had arrested was a major middleweight boxing contender! That got me a lot of attention. In fact, the story of that arrest was featured in one of the city's big newspapers.

I had never planned it out that way, of course, but, looking back, it really was a great news story. Here was this major contender for an international boxing title who'd made the mistake of bringing a gun into the subway ... and here was this petite rookie officer who brought him in and had him locked up. I heard a lot of good-natured jokes after that story ran, jokes about whether he could have knocked me out and so on. I always told people he'd just picked the wrong subway to walk into with a gun—which is still how I feel about that incident.

Beyond the positive PR and the rapport within the department I enjoyed after that arrest—and both were significant—the experience was an important one. It gave me a major boost in confidence. It reminded me of something essential, something I had learned and now experienced for myself: it's not necessarily the biggest, tallest, most muscle-bound who are the most effective, but the ones who are the best trained and have the best instincts.

In the military, the size of the person on the front lines isn't going to be what makes the big difference: it's going to be how you're trained, what your instincts are, and how you take action on those. It's the same in a police department. I had plenty of first-hand evidence now that it was my training, my presence and energy that were going to keep me safe when I was out on the streets (or anywhere else, for that matter), and I was quite confident about that now. The fact that I was small no longer made any difference to me. I was exactly where I was supposed to be.

As I write this, I look back on the twenty-one years I spent on the streets and realize I was fortunate to be able to learn very quickly what the job was all about. It was about leveraging your training, your people skills, and your sense of purpose—not so much your potential for using physical force, but your mind, first and foremost. Your goal was to use all your personal resources efficiently enough to make sure you came home the way you left roll call: in one piece. And thank goodness I was always able to do that. Every day I went out, I came back to my locker at the end of the day, in one piece.

*     *     *

There were three big lessons I learned during my first year on the street as a patrol officer. Well, there were a lot more than three important lessons, but these are the three most relevant to this book, which is about police officers and their individual experiences of stress.

First and foremost, I learned the quality of your person-to-person relationship with your partner makes a huge difference to the quality of your work on the street. This is an intense world in which the officers operate; especially the world of the patrol officer, and the ability to rely on someone who not only understands on an intellectual level what you are going through, but has actually experienced it with you, improves what you're able to accomplish when you're out there on patrol. *Only another police officer knows what a police officer goes through.* This is a critical point, one that I'll be examining from a number of different angles in this book. For now, the point I want to make is that once you go out on the street, your ability to come back in one piece often depends on your ability to communicate with your partner.

Second, I learned that all police-work, and especially police-work that involves interaction with the general public, is usually, primarily, about solving problems. Watching television shows about police officers out on patrol, you might get the impression that they are always involved in some dramatic life-and-death struggle with a single criminal … or that they bring some intricate philosophical debate to the table that plays out with criminals or representatives of the court system … or that they are fueled by some personal obsession about justice, or being right, or compensating for personal problems, or whatever else might sound exciting. Any one of those choices might make for a good hour-long television episode, but none of those choices reflect the reality of being an officer on patrol. Out there, you spend most of your time helping people solve problems. You spend time looking for ways to solve those problems in which no one will get hurt—including you and your partner. The big irony here is that officers themselves reach a point where they need some help solving the problems in their own lives: and they often don't get that help.

Third, I learned that my own background in counseling and mental health issues, which had initially seemed far removed from the daily work of the officer, actually put me at a huge advantage when it came to dealing with the realities of the street. People tend to think of police officers—and I was sometimes guilty of this before I entered the Academy—primarily as participants in conflict. There are certainly plenty of opportunities for conflict out there—more conflict, really, than anyone would want to have to deal with on a daily basis. But I quickly learned that the key to doing a good job as a patrol officer usually lies not in confronting people, but in de-escalating conflict situations. That means reading their state of mind and emotion, empathizing with them, and finding points of commonality between you—so you can communicate more clearly with them. Those communication skills are very important parts of being a good counselor, and they turn out to be equally important parts of being a good officer, too. Something like 85% of good police work turns out to be based on how you talk to people. The lesson that empathizing with others was for more important than attempting to establish some kind of dominance over them would also have a major impact on the later phases of my career.

\*     \*     \*

I'm often asked what the most challenging experience was for me during my time as an officer on the street. There were a lot of memorable experiences, but the one that comes to mind most powerfully was a domestic dispute call. I reference it here because it reinforced all three of the critical career lessons I just shared with you.

In June 1995 we were called to a family conflict in a tenement building. The individual who answered the door was belligerent from the very beginning. This fellow said, "Go on, get out of here. We don't need you here. We didn't call the police." My partner and I were trying to explain that, even though he hadn't called the problem in, some of his neighbors had called about a male and female arguing.

I took the lead in the discussion, and as I did so, I evaluated his state of mind and emotion. I told him we wanted to come inside, just to make sure everything was okay. Basically, I was trying to reason with him. I made the point that he could lose his apartment, and maybe even go to jail, if he didn't let us in. But he just got more aggressive and wouldn't let us in the door.

Now, as this was going on, we heard a female from another room saying, "Let them in, let them in, let them in." And I noticed, from my angle, that there was a gun on a counter. My partner couldn't see that. So I made a couple of quick decisions.

First of all, I could tell that this person, was disturbed and was not about to be reasoned with; he was impaired somehow, due to drugs or alcohol, and no amount of discussion was going to resolve this. What's more, we were now looking at a situation where there was a weapon involved. In a split-second, as I processed this information, the individual made a move as though he were going to take a swing at my partner.

Three things happened, and they happened very quickly. First, I sent my partner a nonverbal physical signal to let him know that there was a weapon in the room. Second, my partner pushed through the door and quickly subdued the individual. Third, I made my way to the back room where we had heard the voice saying "Let them in." I found a woman —tied to a bed.

What he was going to do to her, I don't even know. But I do know that she said, "Thank God you came in here." She told us he had been drinking heavily and was using multiple drugs that made him unstable and potentially violent. She thought she was going to die.

She made it through that crazy experience unhurt; the gentleman who had been threatening her was brought into custody; and my partner and I got back at the end of the day in one piece. Those were three very good outcomes. Why did they happen? I think it was because my partner and I had the ability to communicate well with each other; because my counseling background made it clear to me very quickly that this was a person who was potentially dangerous; and because we were pretty good by then at looking for ways to solve the various problems we encountered on the street. So yes, those were three pretty important career lessons for me.

Out there, on the street, you are a whole lot of things before you're an arresting officer. You're a communicator. You're a judge. You're a social worker. You're a family therapist. You're an advocate. You are actually playing lots of different roles, and dealing with lots of different situations, before you get to the point of deciding who's going to be arrested, and for what. That's a point a lot of people outside of law enforcement lose sight of.

> *It is reasonable that everyone who*
> *asks justice should do justice.*
> —THOMAS JEFFERSON

\*          \*          \*

My career moved forward pretty rapidly, and in the year 2000, I made sergeant. That was worthy of note, because, again, at this time there weren't that many females and minorities in the pipeline.

I had just enrolled in a Ph. D program in Human Services Marriage and Family Therapy.

My first day out as a newly promoted police sergeant was an eventful one. I was out in a blue-and-white patrol car on a beautiful fall day, working a very rough area of Brooklyn. I had a driver who knew that particular precinct well (I didn't). My partner, a fellow sergeant, had asked, "Hey Deb, would you mind taking the patrol car out today?" For my part, I was looking forward to getting out there and checking in with the officers. I figured, "Okay who am I to say no? He's the veteran sergeant here. If he wants to stay in, let him stay in. No problem.

I'll go out, learn about the community, see what's going on. It's a Sunday; it should be slow."

It turned out to be anything but slow.

My first tour of duty as a sergeant was from seven in the morning until three-thirty in the afternoon. Most of the day was totally uneventful, just what you'd expect on a Sunday. I guess everybody was in watching football on TV (there was a big game on that day). At about three o'clock, I told the driver, "You know what? We've been out here for a while. Nothing's happening. I think we should start thinking about heading back now." It seemed the end of a totally uneventful day was in sight.

Then I heard gunshots.

I turned to the driver and said, "Did you hear that?"

I guess he was looking forward to getting home because he said, "Hear what?"

"Didn't you just hear gunshots?"

He said, "Nah, those weren't gunshots. Those were fireworks."

"Fireworks?" I said. "On a Sunday afternoon? I don't think so. Those were gunshots, and they were coming from up the block there. Why don't we drive up there and see what's going on?"

"You sure?"

"Yeah, I'm sure. I've been on the job long enough, I think I know what gunshots sounds like."

He turned the car around and we headed for the sound. Lo and behold, as we're driving our car up the street, we see an individual running towards us, firing a revolver.

I figured out later that this was a drug deal gone bad, and that the person I saw was actually shooting *at* someone. What I took in at first, though, was what it looked like: that he was shooting at random—in an area where civilians could be hurt or killed—and that he just plain did not know whether or not there was a police cruiser in his field vision. I mean this man had tunnel-vision. I don't think he even saw the big blue and white vehicle we were in. We were driving right towards him, and he just kept firing.

As I say, he was shooting, not at us, but at another individual; this person happened to be running in our direction. Now, we were sitting in the car, and here was this person shooting in our direction. Part of me was thinking, "I can't believe this is happening." And another part of me said, "You've got to get out of the car and arrest this guy."

The second voice—the voice of instinct, the voice of training—took over. Before I really knew what was happening, I had opened the door, jumped out of the car and started chasing the shooter. He was right in front of me. He made eye contact with me. And a split-second later, before I could get any words out, this guy shot his intended victim straight through the heart. The victim was dead in seconds. We later learned he was someone who owed this drug dealer money.

Now what?

I still couldn't quite believe what had happened—it's not every day that someone looks a police officer right in the eye and then turns around and shoots someone—but there wasn't a lot of time to think about all of that. The shooter started running.

I chased him. My driver stopped the car, jumped out and ran behind me. We both had our guns drawn.

We faced an interesting situation. Here was someone who was armed, an obvious danger to others, but who had turned his back to us to run away. That means he wasn't aiming directly at us and did not pose an immediate threat to us. In that situation, you're not supposed to use deadly force.

So I didn't. I did what I was supposed to do. I shouted, "POLICE. DON'T MOVE!"

Believe it or not, he stopped in his tracks. I could hardly believe it myself.

Within about a second, we had him on the ground, our guns pointed at his head. And about a second after that, we had him cuffed.

That was a pretty interesting first day as a sergeant!

I eventually won the Brooklyn District Attorney's Law Enforcement Award for apprehending that individual without incident. *Without incident* means we didn't shoot back at him ... when a lot of other officers might have.

What I learned from that experience was initially hard to describe, but in the years since, I've become better at telling others the two things that memorable arrest taught me about police work.

First, it was a powerful reminder that things can happen instantaneously. You can go from boredom to being in a life-threatening situation in just a few seconds. This experience was certainly proof of that. We were preparing to wind down our day, go inside and find out what the score of the football game was—and then, POW! The next thing you know, I'm outside the car with my gun drawn, and someone is being shot right in front of me.

I had known on an intellectual level that things could unfold very quickly, and very dangerously, out on the street, and I had been trained well to respond to that danger. Now I knew the danger in my own nervous system from direct experience. I also knew I could maintain my self-control in a dangerous situation like that and make good decisions. You have to be in control of the situation. This is not a television show. You can't start randomly firing back at the guy and causing unnecessary risk to the public if the threat is no longer there. You can't let yourself get overwhelmed by the sudden rush of events. That's what happens sometimes with a lot of neophyte police officers. They become overwhelmed, they hear gunshots and they stop making good decisions. They forget that it's Sunday afternoon and there are children and elderly people out on the street with them. They just start shooting. You still have an obligation to make good decisions, even if you are adjusting to a situation you didn't expect.

And the second big thing I learned that amazing day was that I was just like everybody else who goes through an extremely difficult and potentially traumatic situation. It was stressful. It took me off center, and I had to use some coping strategies to get myself back to a state where I was calm and resourceful and ready to do a great job again.

That was important for me to notice because I'd always been the one who was caught up in the role of helping other people. Now, here I was in a situation where I had to use some of my own advice to get to a healthy place where I could move on from the situation and feel ready to go back on the street. Just being able to talk about what I had gone through with other officers turned out to be extremely important.

That shouldn't have come as any surprise, and I guess it was reassuring in a way to be reminded that I was just like every other officer out there. In order to move past that event, I had to do what I knew everyone else had to do. I had to talk about it. I had to share what I had gone through with other officers. I knew it was healthy for police officers to do that after seeing a homicide in person, and it was a good experience to realize that it was healthy for me to do that, too.

Every officer who has worked on the street has incredible stories like that to share, and it's important to be reminded now and then about how vital it is to share your story when something dramatic like that happens to you. You can't keep it bottled up. You're just not tough enough to keep it all closed inside. Nobody is you. You should talk to other officers about it and interact with people who have been through the same kinds of things you've been through (though not, of course, the exact same events). You have to share what happened to you. You have to bounce it around and get in front of people who can listen to what happened.

I thought I was giving all that good advice to myself after that intense experience on the street. And I was. But (without realizing it) I was also practicing sharing that advice with other officers.

# CHAPTER FOUR

## Peer To Peer

*There is a tonic strength, in the hour of sorrow and affliction, in ... getting back to the simple duties and interests we have slighted and forgotten. Our world grows smaller, but it grows dearer and greater.*

—WILLIAM GEORGE JORDAN

I had been a patrol officer for about seven years when I finally completed my Masters degree. ( I went on to earn my Ph. D in 2004.) At that point, I caught a big break.

One of the truly great things about the New York City Police Department is that it keeps track of the skills and aptitudes its people develop, and then tries to match its people with the right next step in their career, based on what they've accomplished and learned most recently. That's what happened to me. My superior, Mike Ryan, heard that I had received my degree and called me into his office.

"I want you to go inside," he said. "I think it's the right thing for you, and the right thing for the department, too. I think you could help a lot of officers."

By *go inside*, he meant I should stop being a patrol officer and start counseling full-time. And the moment he said that, I resisted it—more because I *saw* myself as a patrol officer than for any other reason.

"I don't know," I said. "I'm pretty good at what I do."

"Moore," he said, "it's been seven years now. What the hell are you doing still playing cops and robbers out there? Take a day to think about this. Sleep on it. Why don't you put that fancy degree of yours to work on yourself tonight? Don't you feel yourself a more little burned out at the end of the day, a little less ready to give it your best shot every morning? Take a deep breath before you turn this down. You were born to do this."

I went home and thought about it, as he'd instructed.

And when I was done, I realized he was right.

It really had been force of habit that told me to turn the assignment down; the sheer familiarity of thinking of myself as a patrol officer. The reality was that I was beginning to do what I had seen a lot of officers do: burn out. I was losing my edge. After thinking about it for a long time, I concluded that seven years on the street was probably enough for anyone, and certainly enough for me. It was time to move my career to the next level … and act on the intention that had been burning inside me for a long time: to help people in law enforcement, and to do research on police stress and help cops learn how to cope with it.

It felt like the right next step because I always had an interest in helping people. When I was out on patrol, I was helping people in a law enforcement capacity. Now it was time to look at helping officers in a teaching and counseling role. I would be helping the helpers.

I have to acknowledge here just how lucky I was to be working in an organization that regularly asked, "What's the strength here? What have you been studying? What have you added to your portfolio since we last looked at this? Where does your career need to go next?" When you've got someone who's ready to have that discussion with you—and I certainly did at the NYPD—then you're very fortunate. I was fortunate. I had someone who was looking out for me. And the truth was, even though this career change was not my idea, it was just what I needed. I was on a path headed toward burnout, and fortunately, Mike Ryan picked up on that.

I had a smooth transition. I was able to put everything I had learned into place and use it to assist others.

Most people, whose exposure to police work consists of watching cop shows on TV, don't realize how much goes on in a big-city police department. There's a whole lot that happens besides going out on patrol, which is pretty much all civilians see. But I knew I was part of a city agency that had over 38,000 sworn officers. And I knew there was a lot of room for going into different units and details.

We agreed that it made the most sense for me to start out in education rather than moving directly into counseling. It would be a good transitional step. I wanted to learn as much as I possibly could about the department and the incoming classes of rookies I would be teaching. It didn't seem like that long ago I had been a rookie myself!

I was teaching them law, which was pretty interesting because I didn't have a formal law background—although, of course, I certainly had a lot of practical experience when it came to staying on the right side of the law as an officer on the street. Law was the only opportunity open at the time, and the chief really wanted me to come work for him. So I did my homework and started out teaching law.

Once an opportunity opened up, they placed me in the counseling unit where I worked directly with new recruits—the same group I had gotten used to teaching. That was interesting, because working with recruits means working with a different type of stress than you would when working with a seasoned officer. As you might imagine, the stress recruits experienced was centered on dealing with the transition period between being a civilian and going into the Police Academy. They had a lot of new things to learn in a very short period of time, and they had a lot of disruptions from family life to deal with. And of course, they had to deal with the stress of the unknown. I remembered all of that well enough.

Today, after all of the work I've done counseling officers (both in one- on- one and group settings) and researching the kinds of stress they experience on a personal level, that initial experience of counseling the new recruits seems quite small on the landscape now. Having said that, it was one of the major turning points in my career, and I will tell you why. When it came to helping these recruits, my own direct experience as a recruit just entering the Police Academy turned out to be at least as important as any formal training I'd received. When I talked to them about what they could expect to have to deal with at the Academy, and how best to deal with it, they knew I wasn't just spouting some kind of abstract theory. I had been through the same experience and come out the other side. That meant they were more likely to listen to me than they were to someone who hadn't been through the Academy.

I had an automatic position of commonality with those recruits, and that helped me implement the formal counseling techniques I had spent so much time studying. In fact, I was in a much better position to implement what I had learned ... **because I was a member of the group I was counseling. I was one of them. And that's what made the difference.**

They were more willing to let me in because I was one

of them, and I was in an ideal position to help them build a positive self-image as an officer-in-training, and eventually as an officer, because of the shared experience base we had. We were able to see the best in each other, more or less instantly, because of that shared experience. And that process began by **being one of them.**

*The most effective way to achieve right relations with any living thing is to look for the best in it, and then help that best into the fullest expression.*
—ALLEN BOONE

One of the critical things I was reminded of very quickly once I moved over to the Counseling Unit and began counseling active duty NYPD officers was the double reality of police stress.

I had experienced this double reality first hand when I was out on the street, and now I was seeing that same double reality play out in the lives of patrol officers. What I'm saying may sound a little confusing to an outsider, but I think that anyone who has done police work can tell you there are two very different kinds of stressors for the brave people who do these jobs: internal and external.

The kind of police stress that most civilians are used to thinking about—typically from watching news programs and cop shows on TV—is the external kind. By external, I mean something that happens to you that is outside of your home life and outside of the department: my experience watching a homicide and arresting the perpetrator, for instance. This is the stuff that is the most dramatic and vivid, the stuff civilians typically asked you about.

What comes as a surprise to a lot of people who aren't active officers is how potentially debilitating internal stressor can be. These are the stressors that take place inside your home and inside the department. These are typically stressors related to relationships and family problems, or working schedules, or the need for time off, or personnel matters like compensation or promotion, or conflicts with peers or superiors.

The external stressors—high-profile arrests, traumatic experiences on the street—are flashier and likelier to wind up on the evening news than the things that happen at home and inside the department. But those internal stressors—long hours, time away from loved ones, promotion an officer wanted but didn't get—are actually the stressors that tend to cause the bigger challenges for officers.

This comes as a surprise to a lot of people outside the law enforcement environment, but when you stop to think about it, you will realize that it's really not all that surprising. Internal stressors are more of an everyday experience, and they may fester unaddressed for months, or even years, and combine with other stressors in complicated ways.

All of this makes the job of the counselor, whose job it is to "help the helper", more challenging. As a general rule, counselors must be prepared to spend more time tracking down internal stressors than they do tracking down external ones. After all, the officer who goes through a difficult and potentially traumatic experience on the streets is usually big news inside the department. That means he or she is on your counseling "radar screen" more or less instantly; you probably know you have to help him or her deal with, and process, what has happened. But the officer who is having problems at home, or who has a major communication

obstacle with a commanding officer, or who is dealing with stress related to being gay in an institution
that is primarily straight—that officer is more difficult
to identify and help. This is a big challenge, because
those kinds of internal stressors are typically the ones
that are most likely to cause burnout and early departure from the force.

So: how do you handle this challenge? In many cases, the counselor can make a good start just by being
willing to listen at length to someone who's close to
an officer. These friends and loved ones are likely to be
the ones who have seen, first-hand, the problems of an
officer who is dealing with an internal stressor. A very
big part of this job is being open to, and listening carefully to, colleagues and family members. Let's face it:
typically, police officers are not the kind of people who
come knocking on your door to tell you they need help.
Being open to discussions with all the people in an officer's circle can give you access to a kind of early warning system.

The good thing about that kind of early warning system is that you do get face-to-face with someone who
really needs your help. The more challenging aspect is

that friends and family members typically don't reach out to you at the very early stages of an officer's problem with an internal stressor. Usually, they wait until major problem begins to surface. In my case, that meant that, by the time I saw a police officer who was dealing with a major internal stressor, he or she was seriously out of balance.

Typically, these officers could not see past their difficult current situation. They weren't capable of balancing out their lives because they were in a critical or traumatic period. Very often, these officers perceived that they were at rock bottom, and sometimes they had convinced themselves nothing else could be done.

*"Come back!" the Caterpillar called after her.*
*"I've something important to say."*
*This sounded promising, certainly. Alice turned*
*and came back again.*
*"Keep your temper," said the Caterpillar."*
—LEWIS CARROLL, *Alice's Adventures in*
*Wonderland & Through the Looking-Glass*

The counseling process is all about helping people regain a natural sense of balance in their lives. In the old days, people used to describe this balance as "temperance," a word that now sounds old-fashioned. But if you go to the dictionary, you will find that "temperance" means "moderation in regard to passions, appetites, and emotions" (Dictionary.com). The word comes from the Latin root *temperare*, which means "to divide or proportion duly; to mingle in due proportion; to regulate; to be moderate." To "keep one's temper," then, simply means to experience moderation and balance in life.

In generating counseling examples for this book, I had to think carefully about the many officers I worked with during my years of peer counseling. Because of confidentiality restrictions, I decided to combine the details of several officers from my early years of counseling into one composite narrative about an officer whom I will call "Jack." What follows, then, is "Jack's story," a story that didn't happen in terms of its specifics exactly as I have laid it out, but did happen on an emotional level to a number of officers. Jack's story respects the privacy of the officers I was privileged to help, but also reflects the reality of the challenges we counselors often face when we begin the difficult task of helping the helper.

**I choose to share Jack's story here as this book's first examination of the "how to" of peer counseling, to emphasize a particularly important point: life stories help us to understand the individual.** Each of us has a story. I had to learn—and listen to—Jack's. Each new counseling relationship is a new commitment to draw out a new story, and a new opportunity to listen to that story. Once you have understood a person by listening to his or her story, you can implement an effective counseling process. It doesn't work as well if you try to do it the other way around. So think of this first real-life counseling example in my book as a case study, not of a specific officer, but of the neglected art of uncovering the personal story. That may be the most important counseling lesson of all.

\*        \*        \*

Jack had been on the force for eight years. The sergeant, to whom he reported, referred him to me. His sergeant reported that his productivity was down. He had frequent absences, whereas earlier, he had hardly been absent at all. He often showed up late for work, but had once been among the least tardy officers.

When asked to explain the change, Jack gave his sergeant lame excuses (these excuses, of course, were not Jack's "real story").

For most of his career, Jack had been known as a gregarious person, but now he was quiet and reserved. His peers noticed that something was wrong and reached out to his sergeant, who, in turn, reached out to me.

The word in Jack's unit was that he was having problems with his wife. The sergeant didn't know about any of that, and what's more, he didn't really want to know whether these rumors were true. He was concerned about Jack, though, and wanted him to get better.

The first big challenge for a counselor in a situation like this is to establish rapport. The officers who find themselves being referred for counseling (rather than seeking out counseling voluntarily) are usually angry and frustrated the moment they walk in the door. They're wondering how all of this is going to affect their reputation and career. They don't want to be sitting in a room with a counselor. And they don't want the stigma that sometimes accompanies being reassigned to a desk job.

That was how it was with Jack. He showed up with a frown on his face and sat down in a way that said: "I'm not giving an inch." His arms were crossed tightly. Initially, he wouldn't make eye contact. He had walked in the door, as ordered, but he was, initially, as unwilling to share the "real story" with me as he had been with everyone else.

At this point I should say something about my attire. I was dressed as a civilian. This is standard operating procedure. Counselors generally don't dress in uniform because first impressions are extremely important. We don't want people thinking they are facing some sort of disciplinary action the second they step in the door, which is often the impression a uniform conveys.

This approach to attire, though, has both an advantage and a disadvantage when it comes to getting people to share the real story. The advantage is that some officers relax when they realize they're not in trouble. The disadvantage is that other officers tense up when they think they're dealing with a civilian—someone who doesn't understand them. This was the case with Jack, so it was particularly important that I made it clear that he and I were on the same team.

I was a sergeant back then, so I quickly introduced myself as Sergeant Moore. I explained that I had fifteen years of experience on the force, and had been a patrol officer like Jack, and was called by Jack's sergeant because of the large number of emergency days off Jack had taken in recent months.

These few seconds of introduction led to instant improvements in Jack's demeanor and body language. He no longer had to worry about whether or not I would be capable of understanding his situation because he knew I was a fellow officer. And he didn't have to worry quite as much about whether or not I thought he was crazy, or would tell anyone else he was crazy, because I had made it clear the reason for our visit was his large number of absences—an administrative matter.

At this point I shared with Jack a couple of important points about my role and my responsibilities. I shared with him the same ground rules I shared with any officer with whom I was beginning a counseling relationship. First and foremost, letting him know that if he told me he had any plans to harm himself, there would be no alternative but to refer him to someone else, take away his gun, and remove him from active duty. Under that circumstance—the threat to hurt himself—our confidentiality was limited. Jack understood me, and my being up-front about this appeared to help him relax and become more comfortable. Once his body language relaxed a little further, I knew we were on solid ground.

Jack now knew that he was dealing with a peer, felt safe, and knew exactly what the ground rules were. Now that those rules were out of the way, the conversation began moving smoothly. This is what usually happens with such referrals: you have just a minute or two to set the ground rules, establish commonality, and make the officer feel safe. If you do that, the rest of the session goes well for both of you. If you don't, then you are probably not going to accomplish much: the walls go up. In this case, the walls came down. I was fortunate enough to get Jack to relax and open up to me at the very beginning of our first meeting.

Once the walls came down—a step I emphasize here because without it, literally nothing else constructive is possible within the counseling relationship—Jack and I were ready to have a respectful, supportive discussion between peers about what was really going on in his life.

My job now is to give you a sense of what the initial phase of that respectful conversation sounded like. Please note that, in what follows, I am condensing what takes place in a counseling relationship pretty aggressively. Although it may sound like one conversation, this first phase of this discussion actually took us a number of sessions (after the first session, I called his sergeant with some recommendations; I will share them with you in a moment).

The first, and perhaps most important, discovery for me was that Jack was just as concerned as I was about the negative impact of his being "tuned out" at work, which is what he said was happening to him. He knew there was a problem, and he wanted to find a way to solve it.

This was a major advantage, one I didn't always have in dealing with officers who were facing unbalanced situations in their lives (in cases involving alcohol abuse, for instance, there is often a substantial stage of denial to deal with). In this case, we both acknowledged early on that there was a problem, and we were both looking for solutions.

We returned to the subject of the large number of emergency days he had used up in such a short period of time. Without any hesitation, Jack told me he was having major difficulties with his wife, and, as a result, was finding it hard to focus on the day-to-day responsibilities of his job.

Jack told me he was distracted because he was busy thinking about his wife and son, both of whom were now staying at his wife's parents' home. Their departure had shocked him deeply, and he often found himself thinking of them and neglecting other parts of the job he knew he should be monitoring closely. For instance, while on patrol with his partner, he repeatedly found himself missing key transmissions that came over the police radio.

These incidents alarmed him because he knew they put both his partner and the public—not to mention himself—in potential danger. As a result, on days when he knew he would not be able to focus properly, he called in and told his supervisor (correctly, he felt) that he was dealing with a personal emergency. That excuse might have sounded lame to his supervisor, Jack told me, but it was true, and using it was better than coming to work when he knew he couldn't do his job well.

What bothered Jack was something that wasn't about to go away: his wife had left him, taking their four-year old son. She has left because, Jack said, she couldn't stand his crazy schedules any more.

Jack was an officer who had not yet been able to get settled into a routine tour. That meant his schedule was totally unpredictable. One week, he might be working from 7 A.M. to 3 P.M., and the next from midnight to 8 A.M.. Sometimes he had unexpected overtime. Sometimes he had to attend events and handle crowd control. There was just no way to tell what his week was going to look like ahead of time. Very often, when he came home after a long shift, his wife and son were fast asleep. He would go to bed exhausted and when he woke up, they might be getting ready for bed themselves.

Not surprisingly, Jack's wife had complained about this. Jack had made many attempts to address Janice's concerns. He told me he couldn't count how many requests he'd made to higher-ups in the department to secure a more predictable schedule. He had begged Janice to be patient. And he had reminded her many times, sometimes more tactfully than others, that he had been totally honest with her at the beginning and warned her that a police officer's hours were unpredictable. None of that mattered. She was gone, their marriage had failed, and Jack felt like a failure. I watched as he burst into tears. It was important to let him process that difficult moment without intervening.

His wife, he explained after pulling himself together, had eventually grown tired of their lifestyle. So she had done what she had threatened to do so many times: she had walked away from the marriage. Jack, who came from a family that valued staying together as man and wife over almost any alternative, simply did not know how to deal with the situation. He displayed all the classic signs of depression: difficulty sleeping, no participation in leisure activities, a noticeable downward shift in his patterns of socialization, and the decision to spend a lot of time alone. His life was frighteningly simple: he went to work, came home, slept. It became an endlessly repeated cycle, broken only by the days he knew he was too fragmented and distracted to work without endangering himself or others while on patrol. Jack wasn't sure what happened to him, and he certainly didn't know what to do about it, but he knew he didn't like it. He was distraught.

At first I was quite concerned about the depression. Very often, when you deal with officers who are experiencing depression, you find a potential for suicide or other self-destructive behavior. It didn't take long, however, for me to conclude this was not a real danger in Jack's case. He wasn't out to hurt himself. He was just trying to figure out what happened and find a way to deal with it.

When I asked him why he felt he was tuning out at work, Jack explained that the answer was simple: he missed his wife and son and spent a lot of time thinking about them. If the police radio sent a message and Jack was busy thinking about what his wife or son might be doing, he might not notice the radio at all.

I called Jack's supervisor after our first session and asked whether he would consider letting Jack do a lower-priority job when he felt like he needed to be off patrol duty. That would mean following Jack's lead and letting him decide when it made more sense for him to perform a duty, such as checking in prisoners or searching them, instead of riding in a squad car with his partner. It would also mean keeping this ongoing reassignment relatively low key, and recognizing it wouldn't help Jack, or anyone else, to have the whole department talking about his troubles. Jack's superior agreed. That arrangement was fairer to everyone: Jack, his partner, and the public. Perhaps best of all, it took a lot of pressure off Jack.

\*     \*     \*

My sessions with Jack continued for about five months. Over time, we worked together to Identify a major stumbling block: Jack viewed the end of his marriage as an indication of his own failure as a person. This viewpoint had taken his life out of balance.

Every day he woke up and did not see his wife, he concluded that he had somehow ceased to exist. When the marriage ended, a part of Jack was convinced that he had ended. Jack's family influences, which included plenty of examples of people "sticking it out" no matter how difficult the problems in a marriage became, was a major cause of this response.

We spent a fair amount of time creating a new set of references that made it easier for Jack to decide his life was not over because his marriage had ended. As part of that work, I gave Jack an assignment that involved socializing with other people, an assignment based on a remark he made in passing about having been on a bowling team in college. Once a week, we agreed, Jack had to go bowling with at least two friends. This was a non-negotiable aspect of his counseling, something that he had to take personal responsibility for committing to, and completing, between our sessions together. He did, and he found he enjoyed the bowling quite a bit more than he had expected to.

When I first got a sense of how deep Jack's depression was, I felt it was a very real possibility we might need to reach out and schedule some sessions with another professional and explore the possibility of setting up a medication program to help Jack do a better job of functioning on a day-to-day basis. I mentioned this possibility to Jack at the beginning of our sessions, and told him it might become something we needed to consider. As it happened, though, he did not need this referral, was able to make a full readjustment, regain his balance and resume his active role as a patrol officer.

Jack's personal experience of stress was, of course, unique to him ... but it was also emblematic of the debilitating stress I have encountered in countless officers over the years. Each of us has our own issues with regard to stress. And each of us faces the same challenge: finding how to handle that stress in a way that restores balance to our lives and our careers.

Stress is "hardwired" into the lifestyle of the urban police officer—and, all too often, into the lives of his or her family members. In fact, the job is widely regarded as one of most stressful our society has to offer, an assessment that is hard to challenge when one considers the high incidence of divorce, drug and alcohol abuse, and suicide that correlates statistically to those who pursue this career. Stress is ubiquitous in many professions. To identify a job whose chronic exposure to intense, daily, potentially crushing stress is comparable to the impact police work has on the officer and their loved ones, we must move past job titles like firefighters, airline pilot and brain surgeon and consider such posts as a prison guard in a high-security facility. That's the closest domestic equivalent, I believe. Also, members of the military engaged in combat overseas are the only people I can think of whose work exposure routinely exceeds the stress levels experienced on and off duty by an urban police officer, and they present a special case. Combat personnel are, of course, likely to experience more profound and more debilitating experiences of stress than a police officer. Yet their careers typically do not encompass a high stress level for a period of a decade or more, as a police officer's can. The strains and tensions of law enforcement, especially urban law enforcement, is unique, extreme, and, very often, impossible to avoid.

Those who have accepted the responsibility to help officers whose lives have become, for whatever reason, deeply unbalanced (as Jack's was) must help those officers find constructive ways to address stress issues. Such issues are likely to present uniquely in each officer's life, be specific to work in law enforcement, and broadly predictable within certain categories. Stress can be identified strongly with problems at home, as it was in Jack's case. It can be correlated with work-related experiences such as an officer's constant exposure to violence, suffering, trauma and death, or to a particularly difficult case involving such disturbing factors as homicide or child abuse. Stress can also be connected to complex patterns of dysfunction that play out across the "on-duty" and "off-duty" worlds simultaneously. Indeed, stress tends to be cyclical: experiences in the home realm tend to magnify an officer's vulnerabilities to stress experiences in the on-duty realm, and vice versa.

Contributing factors to debilitating stress may build up over time from events that might not seem, to an outsider, to be all that stressful. For instance, officers who deal with offenders on a daily basis may experience a judge's verdict in a particular case as deeply stressful, an experience that may be mystifying to those who are close to the officer, but may make more sense to a fellow officer who has seen many lenient sentences handed down over the years. Similarly, police officers who perceive the public's attitude toward the police as unfavorable may, after a long period, experience a particular incident of disrespect from the public as deeply stressful.

Interestingly, the nature of the organization in which an officer works may be the most serious source of stress. Historically, police departments have been structured as quasi-military operations, with top-down command structures. This state of affairs, which is neither more nor less than a fact of life an officer must accept when committing to a career that involves police work, typically results in a work environment that is rigid, inflexible, and bureaucratic when it comes to accommodating the scheduling, therapeutic, promotional, or assignment needs of individual officers. Opportunity for advancement is often limited, and despite the ubiquity of the personal computer, a vast amount of paperwork is still required. In some departments, the leadership remains predominantly white, male, heterosexual, and insular, a factor that in and of itself serves as a cause of stress for many officers. Comparatively few departments are changing these cultural dynamics, but the pace needs to quicken. A peer counselor must, in many cases, be willing to advocate for internal decisions that will help officers address such "internal" stressors, which I will examine in more detail later in this book.

Recognizing and understanding stress is the first defense in handling it. The second defense involves developing specific coping strategies, which I will examine in chapter seven. A peer counselor can help in both areas. The two-tiered goal of effective peer counselors—and other care professionals, for that matter—is first, to work with officers to help them recognize the nature of the stress they are experiencing and second, to apply the best adaptive coping mechanisms. This is what happens in every successful counseling experience (including mine with Jack).

The resourcefulness with which officers and their counselors learn to cope with stress will determine whether their overall response and outcome will be successful or not. My experience has been that, collectively, officers have good coping skills when it comes to supporting each other and managing stress in their work environments. A lot of potential and benefit can come from group counseling sessions. Tools to help counselors and therapists to conduct such sessions can be found in Chapter 10 of this book.

Our responses to potentially debilitating stress experiences may not be resourceful at first—Jack's was not—but that should not concern us too much. With time, repetition and support, officers can learn to make better, more constructive and self-preserving responses to stressful situations and circumstances. With help we can help ourselves … and we can, in turn, learn to help others acquire stress management skills.

*The mind can go either direction under stress—toward positive or toward negative: on or off. Think of it as a spectrum whose extremes are unconsciousness at the negative end and hyperconsciousness at the positive end. The way the mind will lean under stress is strongly influenced by training.*

—FRANK HERBERT

# CHAPTER FIVE

## Never The Same

*Post-traumatic stress disorder is a whole-body*
*tragedy, an integral human event of enormous*
*proportions with massive repercussions.*
—SUSAN PEASE BANITT

The event that rocked the world—not just the NYPD's world, not just my world, but everyone's world—was the 9/11 terrorist attack on America. After that attack, things were never the same. It was communal trauma: trauma on a national, local, and personal scale.

New York City—my city—was, of course, one of the

prime targets of that attack. The pain suffered by the people of New York; the lives lost, families broken, bravery from unexpected heroes, and of course the astonishing sacrifices of the police officers, firefighters, and other public safety officials who went above and beyond the call of duty to fulfill their responsibilities as "first responders"—all of these events have been well documented elsewhere so I will not attempt to detail them here. I'm not going to try to make any detailed assessment of my own personal emotional response to the attacks, or the processing I found necessary to come to terms with what happened that day, not because I think these experiences are unimportant, but because I think that is a topic for another book. What I will share here, though, is an important reminder that I drew from that awful day and its long aftermath, a lesson that confirmed an initial instinct I had experienced for some time as a counselor working with officers: to be an officer is, by definition, to serve as a helper to the community ... but every once in a while, the helper needs help, too.

*Who helps the helper?* It was this important question that inspired and motivated me in the phase of my career that involved direct counseling of officers. This was the question that never went away. This was the question, ultimately, that drove me to write this book.

> *Law enforcement officers are never 'off duty.'*
> *They are dedicated public servants who are*
> *sworn to protect public safety at any time and*
> *place that the peace is threatened. They need all*
> *the help that they can get.*
> —BARBARA BOXER

\*     \*     \*

Since so much of what follows in this book is about leadership—either the formal leadership that comes with a change in rank, or the informal, but just as essential, variety of leadership that is required to lead a group of officers in managing stress in a healthy way—it seems appropriate to close this part of the book by sharing how my career with the New York City Police Department concluded. The end of my career was an immensely positive experience for me, and I believe that was so, in no small degree, because of the leadership role I was privileged to take on within the department. When I first entered the NYPD, no one could have convinced me that I would assume a significant leadership role within it. That this seemingly unlikely scenario became a reality is due to a cycle I call the Leadership Imperative, which I'll be discussing in more depth a little later in this book.

*     *     *

After ten years, I got promoted out of my counseling role and took on the duties of a lieutenant. As a lieutenant, I had significantly more managerial responsibility than I had when I was a sergeant. At this stage I was a member of the Department's middle management. I was personally accountable for the actions of about 160 people, mostly officers, but some sergeants as well. Of course, having played both roles myself, I was well aware of the nature of their duties and of the kinds of challenges they faced.

I made the choice to be the kind of lieutenant who spent time out on patrol with the officers. Typically, four out of my five working days were spent on the streets where the action was unfolding and decisions were being made. I spent a lot of time in a supervisor's car; I had a special driver, which felt much different from my days driving in a patrol car with a partner. I logged a lot of miles in that supervisor's car, going from one "hot spot" to another.

Why did I decide on such an active role? I wanted to be sure that, in addition to the administrative work I was responsible for performing, I also had the opportunity to play a peer-to-peer supervisory role in person. I wanted to interact face-to-face with the officers and sergeants for whom I was responsible. I felt that if I expected the sergeants who reported to me to put their "feet on the street" when they were supervising their people—and I did!—then I had an obligation to practice what I preached. I wanted to lead by example, and since the officers I was supposed to lead were spending so much of their time out on the street, that meant to me that I didn't want to spend most of my own time behind a desk.

I truly believe that in order to lead you need to spend time with the people you are supposed to be leading. You have to understand what they experience. You have to go through what they're going through. I realized I had spent a lot of time in a counseling role, and I was very proud of the contributions I had made in that setting. But when it became clear that it was now time to consolidate the work I had done, I had to figure out what the period leading up to my retirement would look like. I decided it was time for me to make a leadership contribution, and that when I did, I would do so by going back to my roots and reminding myself what it meant to be a cop out on patrol. I decided I wanted to be the very best leader I possibly could. That meant I would end my career the way I began it as a rookie fresh out of the Academy: out on patrol.

I made sure I got out there at least four days out of every five. It's important for me to mention that I was not just responding to the calls that came in, not just examining crime scenes with the officers and sergeants I was responsible for, but also interacting with the community, getting to know people, introducing myself and the Department, and making sure that people understood we were all on the same team. In a way, I felt like a big part of my job was to do for another generation what Detective Reynolds had done for me all those years ago when she'd visited my classroom. I shook as many hands as I could, handed out as many business cards as I could, told as many people as I possibly could how to reach the precinct if they ever needed us for anything.

One of the most important takeaways for me during the final period of my career was a duty I already knew about, but one I knew I needed to recommit myself to: **being a leader in the field of law enforcement has an ongoing obligation, not just to the community, but to the officers who support and protect that community.** A leader in our world has to make sure the helpers get the help *they* need, even when (especially when) they don't quite know how to ask for that help. As I approached my final days as an active member of the NYPD, I made a commitment to myself to write down some of the most effective tactics and insights I had developed over the years as a "helper of the helpers," and to make sure that the resources I had refined over the course of a long and satisfying career were made available to police departments across the country. In the next section of this book, you'll find those resources.

# PART II

*Who Helps*
*The Helper?*

# CHAPTER SIX

# Unhealthy Coping Strategies

*Suicide is a permanent solution to a*

*temporary problem.*

—A SURVIVOR OF A

GOLDEN GATE BRIDGE SUICIDE ATTEMPT

J. Edgar Hoover once said: "No amount of law enforcement can solve a problem that goes back to the family." He was right, of course, about a challenge that has faced law enforcement and society at large for decades: the roots of criminal activity. Yet I think Hoover was also talking—perhaps without realizing it—about a challenge that is now recognized as facing every law enforcement body in the United States: the challenge of officers committing suicide as a result of job-related stress. This problem is the gravest and clearest sign of our failure to help those officers who help the community.

As I write these words, the suicide rate among police officers in the United States is more than 50% higher than the rate of suicide in the civilian population (O'Hara and Violanti 2012). Ages thirty-five to thirty-nine appear to be at particularly high risk of suicide, as do officers with between ten and fourteen years on the job (O'Hara and Violanti 2012). No amount of law enforcement—by which I mean no amount of bureaucratic regulation—can change the sad fact that this is a problem that goes back to the family, and one that needs to be discussed openly within the family if it is to be solved. The challenge here is that the problem of suicide goes back to not one, but two kinds of families: the individual families of officers who die by their own hand, and the larger family comprising the rest of the law enforcement community. As members of that family, we have an obligation to ask ourselves: in the past, have we let those

officers down in ways large or small? And if so, how?

> *(Before 2008), no police suicide had ever been documented as having resulted from emotional trauma experienced on the job—they were believed to happen only because of 'personal/family problems,' financial hardship, or moral decay and criminal behavior. The 2008 NSOPS report questioned this thinking, noting that, 'While we cannot yet be certain that police work by and in itself is a suicide risk factor, we can with some assurance state that it serves as a fertile arena for suicide precipitants, including relationship problems, culturally approved alcohol use and maladaptive coping, firearms availability, and exposure to psychologically adverse incidents. Contextually, police work is therefore a probable part of the causal chain of suicide.'*
>
> — O'HARA & VIOLANTI 2012

It is common for experts of various kinds to describe

the epidemic of suicide among active-duty officers as a

tragedy. This label is accurate, of course. It is a tragedy. Yet the most important thing to remember about a tragedy is that is does not come about as the result of random chance.

The very word *tragedy* comes from ancient Greece. If you look closely at how the Greeks described tragedy, you'll notice that *tragedy* is always connected to a mistake made by a human being. So if we want to describe our current suicide figures as a tragedy, that's fine, but we should understand that this label leaves us with an obligation to identify what, exactly, the mistake was, so the tragedy is not repeated in the future.

In this particular tragedy, there is a single mistake we all need to look at very closely. It is the perpetuation of the myth, still all too common in police forces, that acknowledging the existence of emotional problems is not something a "strong" police officer does.

Most officers in most big-city departments still believe that acknowledging such problems to anyone, in any way, in any setting (with the possible exception of a bar, where alcohol may lower some of the social barriers, but presents a whole new set of risk factors) is a sign of weakness. Public knowledge of this *weakness* is believed to destroy, or at least sidetrack, careers. As a result, most officers may get little or no support during times of greatest vulnerability, and may have only ineffective or flawed coping strategies for dealing with the immense stressors that are part of their daily working environment. Too many of these officers are left to solve problems that simply cannot be solved independently. They then descend into dark places from which some never emerge.

Whether we realize it or not, we all share some of the responsibility for this tragedy. Some thoughts on how best to fulfill our responsibility follow.

## Moving Beyond the Stigma

*Our wounds are often the openings into the best and most beautiful part of us.*
—David Richo

As we have seen, chronic stress can be extremely debilitating for police officers. Unfortunately, there is something possibly more debilitating than stress: the potentially lethal stigma that exists in the rank-and-file of most departments against reaching out and asking for help in dealing with stress in a constructive way.

Too many officers believe—and encourage others to believe—that being an effective officer means being a totally *self-contained* officer when it comes to coping with stress. If you can't "handle it" on your own (so the myth goes), then you've picked the wrong job and you are best advised to go find another. Among the commonly accepted signs of not being able to "handle it" is the desire to work with a therapist or other caregiver to refine one's coping strategies. If you need someone else to talk to, many officers believe, that's a sign that you can't "handle it."

However, the exact opposite is true. To be an effective officer, it is absolutely essential to have someone to talk to about what you've experienced. Many of the situations you will face as an officer will place you in a position where the help of a therapist, counselor, or other caregiver will be essential to your personal well-being and your ability to serve and protect the public and your fellow officers. That is the real-world meaning of "handling it:" taking responsibility for your own internal well-being by connecting in a constructive, supportive way with others who can help you process things you are unlikely to be able to process on your own. Yet, in too many departments, the stigma against realizing you need help, the stigma against taking action to get that help, persists as it has persisted for decades. One of the chief reasons I wrote this book was to help overturn that stigma. To perpetuate the stigma, or to let it stand un-challenged, is to sentence countless officers to fight the battle alone—a battle that, in many cases, they cannot expect to win without allies. Yet they fight that losing battle because they have been trained to believe they will be labeled as "unstable" if they seek help for the (prob-ably inevitable) psychological or emotional problems that accompany police work. They have been trained to believe their career will be ruined if others ever perceive them as "weak."

Time and time again, I have seen first-hand that this stigma against seeking help compels officers to develop unsustainable, negative stress-coping strategies, such as alcohol or substance abuse, inappropriate behavior at home that leads to major marital or family problems, and inappropriate behavior at work that leads to disci-plinary action or even legal problems. Time and time again, I have seen the stigma that persuades officers to keep serious problems with stress to themselves in the belief that this constitutes "handling it," lead to tragic outcomes that threaten the officer's physical and mental health: post-traumatic stress disorder, heart attacks, ulcers, and other serious problems. And sadly, I have seen this stigma against reaching out for help begin a cycle of denial that culminates in suicide.

The stigma is a lie. It is a sign of strength to reach out for help when it is clear you need it, not a sign of weakness. And far from being a sign of instability, it is a sign of stability to recognize the intense stressors of police work for what they are—potential threats to oneself, one's partner, one's department, and the public one is sworn to protect—and to take action to counteract those threats before they become serious.

It is time for us to acknowledge openly that the stigma against seeking help is deeply unhealthy, both for officers and the departments that rely on them to perform at peak levels. The stigma must be confronted directly at the department level. It must be discussed openly and forced to the surface, where it can be debunked for good.

Like many such dangerous stigmas, this one is rooted in a lack of hard information. Very often, officers reject even the possibility of getting help without having any understanding of the type of help available to them. In this part of the book, I'll address that very common information gap by offering concise summaries of the types of therapy available to officers, and the people who are qualified to deliver that therapy. **This is information every police officer should know and have regular access to. Departments have a moral and ethical responsibility to ensure they become familiar with it and are updated about it regularly.**

SHARING THE INFORMATION IN
THIS CHAPTER SAVES THE CAREERS
AND LIVES OF OFFICERS.
WITHHOLDING IT SUPPORTS THE
STIGMA AGAINST SEEKING HELP ...
AND COSTS CAREERS AND LIVES!

If we perpetuate, or even tolerate, the stigma against seeking outside help, then we are making a conscious choice to leave officers to deal with significant emotional problems entirely on their own. This usually means reliance on four profoundly unhealthy coping strategies, all of which are detrimental to the officer. The four most common coping strategies for officers who are left to "work it out on their own" are listed below.

*Unhealthy Coping Strategy #1: Cynicism.* This is a generalized attitude of distrust and contempt toward human motives and intentions, coupled with a belief that specific attempts to make a positive impact in a situation are worthless or useless. When officers start to experience an overwhelming amount of unresolved stress, they often resort to cynicism as a way of coping. This usually results in making matters worse for themselves, their families, the department they serve, and the public.

*Unhealthy Coping Strategy #2: Emotional Withdrawal.* This, too, is a coping strategy that tends to worsen the officer's situation. Emotional withdrawal can create and deepen marital problems, leave officers less resourceful when dealing with new and unexpected stressors, and lead to feelings of severe isolation and loneliness.

*Unhealthy Coping Strategy #3: Alcohol and/or substance abuse.* The real-world scale of this coping strategy can be difficult to assess accurately, since officers are, of course, prone to conceal problems they have with drugs or alcohol. According to one study undertaken by Rafilson and Heaton (1995), nearly 85% of emotional problems found in the police profession involve alcoholism.

*Unhealthy Coping Strategy #4: Suicide.* The ultimate unhealthy coping strategy. Many officers turn to suicide when the other coping techniques at their disposal have failed them. They deserve better.

# CHAPTER SEVEN

## *Healthy Coping Strategies*

*Anything that's human is mentionable, and anything that is mentionable can be more manageable. When we can talk about our feelings, they become less overwhelming, less upsetting, and less scary. The people we trust with that important talk can help us know that we are not alone.*

—FRED ROGERS

L ike all human beings, police officers do not heal from stress and emotional problems on their own, but in collaboration with others. What follows is a summary of a technique I developed to help promote that kind of collaborative healing and adjustment. I call it the Emotional, Behavioral, Cognitive Technique, or **E.B.C. Technique,** for short.

Mahatma Gandhi once observed: "Your beliefs become your thoughts; your thoughts become your words; your words become your actions; your actions become your habits; your habits become your values; your values become your destiny." With the E.B.C. Technique, one, two, or three types of coping strategies can be used. According to Gandhi and my technique, we can change what we believe and how we think about the stressors we encounter. We can initiate these changes in belief and thinking in groups of two or more people, one of whom needs to be an empathetic counselor or facilitator. The three types of strategies are as follows.

*Emotional Coping Strategies.* These coping strategies involve our efforts to manage our reactions to the stressor, rather than trying to change those reactions. For instance, if you have been having troubles in your math class for a period of weeks or months, you can accept that you are not likely to get great grades in that particular subject. So you do your best, learn to put things in perspective, and move on.

*Behavioral Coping Strategies.* These strategies involve modifying our own actions or taking whatever external steps are needed to resolve the difficulty. For instance, if you are having difficulties at work with your boss, you can schedule time to talk to your boss about the problem, ask to be transferred, or find another job.

*Cognitive Coping Strategies.* These strategies involve modifying your thinking and how you process information about the stressful situation. This will lead to either a shift in your behavioral coping strategy or emotional coping strategy. It could even lead to shift in both, behavioral and coping strategies. So for instance, suppose someone cuts you off in traffic. Initially, you may feel angry and say, "Who does that clown think he is, cutting me off?" Not necessarily a helpful question. Then let's say you begin to process the situation and you say to yourself, *All right. Why would someone drive like that? Perhaps he's responding to an emergency. Or maybe he's late for work. Who knows? He could have his pregnant wife lying in the back seat, going into labor.* Asking better questions helps us regulate our thoughts about the situation, thus leading to changes in how we feel and respond.

Again, I call this the E.B.C. Technique: emotional, behavioral, cognitive. These three doors lead to the same place: effective stress management.

Through one, two, or perhaps all three of these doors lies the capacity, through interaction with an empathetic counselor, to begin to take a new approach to your situation. Once you identify the right coping strategy—a process that involves discussion with a counselor or facilitator—you can change your thoughts and beliefs about any given stressor. With practice, that change will govern your feelings and actions, and eventually become your new automatic response. Thus, making it possible for you to handle the stress in your life in a constructive and positive manner.

If you think back to Jack's case, and examine these three coping strategies, you will see I employed all three strategies in our sessions together. We changed, through extended discussion and evaluation, his thinking and beliefs about his own sense of self-worth, which he had believed was negated with the end of his marriage and his periods of separation from his child. That's the cognitive strategy (notice this strategy may serve as a pathway to identifying the most effective expressions of the other two strategies). We also found ways for him to process the strong emotional responses he had to losing his marriage, without judging or trying to "edit out" those painful responses. We accepted this was something he would eventually work through, so he could move on. That's the emotional strategy. We also changed his actions—his behaviors—by arranging for him to take time off from his patrol duties. That's the behavioral strategy. Let's look at how this E.B.C. approach played out in some other cases.

## MARY'S STORY

I was asked to talk to a female officer whom we'll call Mary. Mary was 33 years old, she was of Afro-Caribbean descent and spoke (her commanding officer warned me) with a pronounced accent. She was hard to understand. She had served two years with the department. Her supervisor, who sounded exasperated, told me over the phone that all those two years proved to him was that she "just didn't fit into the role."

Mary had won—if that is the word—a reputation as an eccentric in her precinct. No single event stood out in her supervisor's mind as the cause of that reputation. It was more a question of her ideology about police duties. Mary, he explained, simply would not make arrests.

"Ever?" I asked, incredulous. "You mean if she saw a drug deal taking place right in front of her, she wouldn't arrest anyone?"

"Let me correct that. She's made a total of two arrests over the past two years." The precinct captain's voice was sad and low, and it played in measured, careful tones that suggested he had spent a great deal of time attempting to be patient about this.

"On both of those two arrests, a sergeant had to be by her side, holding her hand all the way. On her own, she has made zero arrests. With the care and attention of a superior officer, she's made two arrests. Over two years. And let me tell you something else. Every single officer in this precinct knows those numbers."

Mary's peers, I learned, would regularly make fun of her career arrest total. They would tell mean jokes about her behind her back. They would tell mean jokes about her to her face. They refused to ride on patrol with her. The situation was bad for everyone involved. No one liked the prospect of trusting her while out on the street;

every single officer in the precinct had ostracized her.

The supervisor, knowing all this, decided it was time to give me a call. Would I get together with Mary and see whether there was anything I could do to assist her? Of course, I agreed.

Before I met with Mary, I asked her commanding officer to send me her file. It was filled with observations from Pat's sergeant Jim; a man who clearly did not enjoy working with her. Mary, he reported, refused to write out a summons if the person violating the law fit a certain profile. Mary said repeatedly that she did not want to "harass" certain populations, which the sergeant interpreted as meaning she refused to consider arresting anyone of color. Mary, he wrote, was "not a team player."

All of these observations were in line with what the precinct captain had told me, but all of them (I reminded myself) could conceivably be the result of some kind of long-running chemistry problem between Mary and her sergeant. Even if that were the case, however, the problems with her peers were disquieting. When everyone in the precinct refuses to ride patrol with you, that's a sign something is wrong somewhere along the line.

When I saw her for the first time, I have to admit,

my first thought was, "Is this person really a cop?" She just didn't radiate the authority, the sense of being fully present, of being ready for something, that you get from a seasoned officer. Her uniform was disheveled and her hair was a mess—and this during a meeting with a counselor who also happened to be a superior officer, presumably someone on whom she would want to leave a positive impression! Clearly, there was a problem here.

We spent a few minutes going over my role, the reason I had been asked to help her, and the guidelines of what would happen during our sessions together. Just as I had done with Jack, I built up some rapport by being clear about the ground rules for this relationship. I then asked Mary what she thought was going on at the precinct.

The floodgates opened.

It's hard for me to recall a client who opened up to me more easily or more immediately. It's possible this was because I was a black woman, as she was, and perhaps those commonalities did play a role in our conversations. I have to think, though, that it was at least as important that I took the time to sit down with her, look her in the eyes, and ask her what she thought was going on. So far as I could tell, no one in her precinct had done that—

certainly not the sergeant to whom Mary reported (she told me at one point that he simply avoided interacting with her any more than was absolutely necessary). Here again, I was reminded of the importance of creating a safe space in which to communicate.

Mary told me flat-out, in our very first meeting, she was deeply concerned about the possibility she had made a mistake in becoming a police officer. She knew, she said, that she did not fit in, and she was tired of being humiliated by the other officers. She was seriously considering resigning from the force. Unfortunately, she had a small son to support, and needed the income and benefits her job provided.

After just a few sessions, I was able to share my own perspective with Mary about her situation. It was, I told her, entirely possible that leaving the force might be the right next step for her—but I was not yet convinced this was the situation we faced. It was common, I told her, for officers to experience chemistry problems with certain commanding officers, and even within certain precincts. Some officers, I assured her, took a little longer than others to hit their stride after coming out of the Academy. It was possible a change in surroundings, and commanding officers, might help her make a better adjustment and contribution to the department. Of course, it was also possible we would discover Pat's instinct was correct, and she simply was not cut out to be a police officer. In either case, I told her, I felt she was the best person to make the decision about what to do next in her life.

I wanted to give Mary the benefit of the doubt, and I also wanted to give her a sense of control and autonomy, because it was obvious she'd been through a great deal over the past two years. I could tell she had made many efforts to make her career as a law enforcement officer work. So far, nothing had worked. That had to be both frustrating and stressful.

I started by recommending a Behavioral coping strategy. I changed the actions, and the surroundings that gave rise to those actions. How did I do that? By removing Mary from her present command and getting her assigned to a new one. In a new precinct, with a new commanding officer to report to, she would get a fresh start, and we would both be able to make better choices about what should happen next in her life.

Three months later, Mary showed up for one of our sessions and announced she had made a decision. The decision was not a surprise to me, because I had been in regular contact with her commanding officer at the new precinct. Based on the interactions she had experienced with her new commanding officers and new peers, Mary decided it was time to retire from the force. The same pattern of ostracism had occurred in the new environment. She still felt she was being asked to violate her own core principles when her job as a police officer required she directly, personally confront someone who was clearly engaging in illegal behavior—particularly if this was someone of color. The setting had changed, but her responses had not. It was time to acknowledge reality, she said, and the reality was that she just was not cut out to be an officer. I agreed.

It might be tempting for some to conclude this series of sessions with Mary represented a kind of failure. I disagree. Why? First and foremost, Mary and I were able to determine, in a way that reduced the possibility of hard feelings, conflict, or legal action, that she was not well suited to being an officer in the New York City Police Department. That was a win/win for everyone, especially when you consider how long, unpleasant, and drawn-out the termination process can be. The truth of the matter is that some people simply are not born to be police officers. Who knows how or why they became officers in the first place? In the end, does that really matter? These are real, live people who wind up taking the wrong career path, and the sooner they correct the situation, the better off everyone will be.

In addition, by confirming the same problems with performance and social relationships occurred in an entirely different precinct, I was able to ascertain the root problem lay somewhere in Mary's capacity and aptitude—not in the leadership of the first precinct, or in some deeper cultural challenge for the department. That was important, too.

Yet another reason Mary's counseling process represented a win/win was this: the period of our counseling gave her the chance to arrange the right severance package, and also allowed her to get the help and support she needed from relatives during her transition into another job. That, too, was a positive outcome.

## BRIAN'S STORY

Brian seemed to be on the fast track. He had been a sergeant for three years, quickly moving up the rank to lieutenant in seven years of being on the forces. He had been in his groove, in his comfort zone, as a lieutenant. Then he got a promotion and became captain. Suddenly things became very challenging for him. He reached out to me directly—a rarity among my clients (as we've seen, it's much more common for those in the officer's work environment or family circle to reach out to a counselor first).

At first, Brian was reticent with me. I think he was taken aback by the fact that the counselor he reached out to was in fact a subordinate officer. I was a sergeant at the time, which meant he outranked me. Once again, though, by establishing commonality, establishing the ground rules of our session up front, and providing both a sense of safety and a clear commitment of confidentiality, I was able to help Brian feel comfortable enough to tell me what was going on in his life.

As it turned out, what was going on in Brian's life was an unpredictable and frightening pattern of panic attacks. These are brief episodes of intense, debilitating anxiety marked by disturbing physiological symptoms such as heart palpitations, dizziness, nausea, sweating, and trouble breathing regularly. There was also an inability to focus. Unlike many other experiences of anxiety, panic attacks are not triggered by any specific, identifiable event. They come and go mysteriously, without apparent cause. Brian's typically lasted between ten and fifteen minutes. They had not taken place when he was conducting roll call, but Brian was concerned they would.

He was also facing anxiety about challenges he was having at home. In recent weeks, he had begun experiencing panic attacks there, too. His current coping strategy for attacks in either situation—taking time in a private space until the symptoms passed—had left both his coworkers and his wife feeling disoriented and confused. Brian would be in the middle of a conversation, and would, without warning, have to excuse himself for a few minutes. When he reappeared, he would make no effort to explain what had happened. He didn't feel he *could* explain what had happened. He had no idea what was going on, so he simply changed the subject. This approach had worked fairly well for him at work—so far. But the "disappearing act" (as he described it) had become a significant impediment to good relations with his wife, Rebecca, because she had no explanation from him about why he suddenly had to disengage from a conversation. What had happened to him while he was away, and what had led him to believe it was time to return? The mystery was not helping their relationship.

The approach I took here, over our first few sessions, was to help Brian create Cognitive coping strategies that would help him deal with his situation. The first of these strategies was simply to **normalize** the experience, to help him to come to terms with it as something manageable, something he could handle, something that did not endanger his career, well-being, marriage, or his sense of self.

*normalize (verb): to restore to a normal or accustomed state; to relieve of unnecessary pressure.*

Fortunately, this normalizing process was relatively easy to do in Brian's case. Discussing such panic attacks with a counselor can and should be a very positive experience for most people who experience them. This is because panic attacks are a fairly common phenomenon that do not, in and of themselves, signal a serious mental illness. Sharing this important piece of information with Brian during our very first meeting helped him a great deal, because it gave him a frame of reference for what he was going through. Learning he was not alone, that others had faced the same symptoms he was facing and had overcome them, was a major step forward. It gave Brian evidence he was not facing a problem that could cost him his job, his wife, or both. Some of the concerns racing through his mind while he was having his attacks were valid ones; others, though, were exaggerations that he could learn to move past, just as others had learned to move past them. His career was not over. His colleagues did not hate him or consider him incompetent. His family had not disowned him.

- *2.4 million adult Americans suffer from anxiety panic attacks.*
- *Panic attack symptoms most often begin in late adolescence or early adulthood.*
- *Panic attacks rarely occur in people over the age of 65.*
- *The risk for experiencing panic attack symptoms appears to be inherited.*
- *10% of the population will have a panic attack at one time in their lives.*

SOURCE — THE HEALTH CENTER, N.D.

By teaching Brian how to ask himself better questions about what was happening to him, what the likely causes were, and what he could do about the situations that were the real cause of his attacks, I was able to help him reach a point where he had gained more perspective on his situation. In our sessions, we focused on questions like:

- How am I feeling right now about my new work situation?
- How am I feeling right now about my family life?
- What kinds of changes have I had to deal with in recent months?

The answers to these, and similar, questions helped Brian identify and cope with the stressors he was experiencing. They also opened the door to other cognitive shifts that emerged during our discussion and helped him take advantage of new internal resources. It might seem simplistic, but it is true: the mere act of discussing the issues Brian was facing, the act of talking things through with an impartial person who would not judge him or hold anything he said against him, was a major step forward in developing positive coping skills. These interactions helped Brian to think differently, to begin to form different beliefs about what he was experiencing. Here are some of the questions and answers we uncovered that helped him create a new belief system and new thinking routines.

On the work front, Brian was able to express, apparently for the first time, that he was deeply concerned about how he would manage the new responsibilities he'd taken on. He had, he said, gotten very good at being a sergeant. This was not just his opinion, but the opinion of everyone who had given him performance reviews over the past two years. The truth was, he was not at all enthusiastic about leaving the job he now knew "like the back of (his) hand." As a lieutenant, he had overseen between fifty and sixty sergeants and police officers. He was now responsible for overseeing over two hundred people! Suddenly, he was responsible for everyone. And here he was, a guy who started out seven years ago with no career aspirations beyond being a good officer. The skills he had accumulated over the past two years for managing dozens of officers and sergeants, as a lieutenant, had become second nature to him. They were not *irrelevant* to his current assignment, but he knew they were not, on their own, going to be enough to see him through what he had to do now, and he was deeply concerned. What in the world was he going to do? (In response to that question, I suggested Brian pose another question on a daily basis: *What mentor relationships will help me expand my management skill base?* We identified two or three good candidates, including one person who had already reached out to Brian to offer career support.

On the home front, Brian acknowledged during our discussions, again for the first time to anyone, that he was feeling more distant from his wife Rebecca than he could ever remember feeling. He was the first to admit this was probably because he had made interacting with her less of a priority. He'd spent a lot less time at home in the three months since he'd received his promotion, largely because he did not want to fail in his new assignment. He had logged a lot of hours at the precinct, more weekly hours than at any previous point in their marriage. This meant his communication with his wife had suffered. Brian knew those instances where he had suddenly vanished while in mid-conversation, and then reappeared without explanation, had not helped matters. But how could he tell her about what he was going through? He simply didn't feel comfortable talking to Rebecca about such things, not with "everything she was going through."

"Everything she's going through?" I asked. "What does that mean?"

Complicating Brian's domestic situation was a factor that he hadn't mentioned during our first session: Rebecca had recently told him she was pregnant with their first child. This unexpected development had put a lot more pressure on Brian, who was, as we have seen, already dealing with multiple stressors related to a feeling that he was "responsible for everybody" at work. All of this had given rise to a whole new series of uncomfortable questions, none of which he felt safe exploring with his wife. Had he made a big mistake in even accepting this promotion? Suppose he simply wasn't cut out for this job, and suppose he only came to realize that with certainty after he had already committed himself to this career path? Yes, it would give his wife and his new child more stability, but what if he failed? What if he was let go? What if he had to start all over again in another career? Was he even ready for a family? Suppose he wasn't cut out for fatherhood at all, or suppose he was just ill equipped to deal with it, given all the other responsibilities he had on his plate? Without attempting to answer any of those questions, I suggested Brian consider this one on a daily basis: *Will this situation I'm facing now become easier to deal with in the long run, or more difficult to deal with, if I share how I feel about it with my wife?*

This sobering question gave Brian pause, and eventually led him to conclude, on his own, that he was better off opening himself up more to the one-on-one interactions Rebecca was trying to initiate with him. He decided he could start by explaining he was getting counseling (this was something he had not yet mentioned to Rebecca). After some thought, he determined he could also summarize for her what he had learned, during our sessions, about panic attacks. If all of that went well, he would go on to apologize for his sudden exits from their conversations and describe the panic attacks that had led to them.

In addition to asking some better questions about the challenges I have already described (and the list of challenges was admittedly a long one!), Brian had to deal with a related problem, one that many of the law enforcement professionals I've worked with have had to address: a **self-perpetuating stress cycle.** Stressors in Brian's work life (for instance, the long hours he worked) were now aggravating stressors in his home life (for instance, the feeling of disconnection with his wife), and vice versa, in a cycle that had become frightening and potentially disorienting. To help Brian defuse this extremely common cycle, I asked him to consider two questions whenever he felt stressors stacking up on top of one another: *What happens if I do nothing about this stressful situation?* And, *how have I handled similarly stressful situations at earlier points in my life?* These two questions led to an important discussion about the various resources he had already developed for dealing with stress while out on patrol, but had not used consciously in years. There were quite a few of these, including deep breathing techniques, he had never even considered using to deal with stressful situations that arose at home or while he was in the precinct.

Brian's story illustrates the special power of the Cognitive approach. For some people—not all, but some—changing the way you think about a situation is enough. Just by discussing his issues with someone who was willing to listen without judgment, someone who had no personal stake in his situation, someone who could help him change his initial mental approach to a stressor, Brian was able to adapt successfully to a set of circumstances that had once seemed impossible to him. After two and a half months of weekly sessions, he had begun a routine of asking himself better questions, generating better answers, and changing his own assumptions about himself and the new world in which he operated. A mentor relationship with a captain who had once been his own lieutenant gave him some new leadership tactics and a new sense of confidence on the job. The conversation in which he shared with Rebecca his decision to seek counseling led to a new level of trust and intimacy between them, and also a much more supportive pattern of communication within their marriage. And by giving himself some credit for having dealt successfully with other stressors in his past, he was able to consider not just the downsides, but also the upsides, of the new roles that had presented themselves in his life. These new roles were no longer traps, but opportunities. Brian not only ended up pursuing an extremely successful career within the NYPD—he eventually became a Police Inspector!—

but he also found, to his surprise, that he genuinely enjoyed fatherhood.

## JERRY'S STORY

During my very first meeting with Jerry, barely a half-hour into our session, he asked me for help in putting together a plan that would change how he felt about life.

Jerry, a sergeant with a decade and a half of experience, was one of those people who walked into counseling eager to establish rapport, eager to get his issues out on the table, eager to identify a solution to the problems he saw in his world. He wanted to do whatever needed to be done to make things right again, and the sooner the better (these kinds of proactive clients are out there, but counselors probably shouldn't assume that they're likely to run into such people every single time). Very quickly, Jerry had concluded I would support him and would respect his confidentiality, and so he was eager to get the process started.

When I asked Jerry what concerned him most, he said two huge questions were keeping him up at night. Was his marriage over? And: was his career over?

Like many of the officers I worked with who faced

stressors they had not yet learned how to deal with, Jerry was responding to his situation by catastrophizing. This was obvious to me when he told me what had been on his mind before coming to see me. He was afraid that he would never date again. He knew, just knew, that he would never make lieutenant now. He could never have a normal relationship with anyone after this. Everything was falling apart.

Jerry's commanding officer knew these worst-case assessments did not reflect the "real" Jerry, so he asked me to talk to him. "This just isn't like him," the commanding officer told me. "He's usually a very optimistic guy, the most upbeat guy in the building"

What had happened in Jerry's world to cause him to go from being "the most upbeat guy in the building" to him being able to see only the darkest clouds in his sky? A domestic problem. Jerry's wife, Christina, had lodged a formal complaint of domestic abuse against him. She said he'd slapped her during an argument. He swore he hadn't, that they had only been expressing themselves "at the top of our voices," in Jerry's phrase, during a dispute with Christina about money. In that kind of situation, where it's one person's word against another's, the department takes certain precautionary steps. The officer in question is placed on what is known as a modified assignment—in essence, relegated to desk duty. The officer's weapon is taken away while the complaint works its way through the system. The department has to do this, both to protect potential victims of abuse and to protect itself against liability claims. Officers know that being placed in this position does not mean they have been found guilty of misconduct. Officially, the fact that Jerry had been reassigned had nothing to do with his legal guilt or innocence ... but on an emotional level, it had everything to do with his self-image and his ability to cope.

I didn't know what had actually happened between Jerry and his wife. It's possible that he slapped her; it's possible that only harsh words were exchanged, and that Christina, for whatever reason, had resolved to do the most painful thing to Jerry that she could imagine, which was to put him in the halfway world of reassignment until her accusations worked their way through the system. As that process played itself out, Jerry was a very unhappy man.

My job here was to help Jerry put his experience in context. I wanted to give him access to some emotional and cognitive coping strategies that would help him see his situation with more balance and less panic. I told him as much, and he was quick to follow up on my suggestion. If there were strategies that would help him to feel better, help him to get back on his feet, he wanted to know about them. What did I want him to do?

The path I laid out for Jerry was one that he—and most police officers struggling with emotional issues—would probably not have considered on his own. I suggested he join a training group composed of other officers who were going through the same experience: modified assignment following an accusation of domestic abuse.

Jerry agreed—he was, after all, interested in moving forward, and he had reached a point where he respected my opinion and wanted my guidance. I could tell, though, that sharing his experience with a roomful of other people had not been high on his list of possible solutions. "This isn't group therapy, is it?" he asked, a little nervously. Since there was no therapist involved—only me, a counselor, helping the group members learn to deal constructively with their situations—I could honestly answer, "No." But the reality was that Jerry gained many benefits from that weekly series of training session. For one thing, he was able to see for himself that other officers were dealing with challenges similar to his own; for another, he was able to get support and advice from people who empathized with his predicament, were not out to judge him and wanted to see him get back on his game.

Of course, I had told Jerry in our first session that he was not alone in dealing with this kind of challenge, and had assured him repeatedly that many officers in his situation had come off modified assignments to resume productive, upwardly mobile careers. Jerry, however, needed to hear this from those other officers. When he joined the fourteen-week training session, he put himself in a position to come together in a safe setting with his peers, each of them at a different stage of dealing with his own incident, each of them ready, willing, and able to share experiences, insights, and coping methods.

The result, in just a little more than three months, was a seemingly miraculous change in Jerry's outlook on his marriage, his career, and life in general. Having spent time with a supportive group of men who had gone through more or less the same experience as he, he convinced himself his world was not, in fact, falling apart.

The group approach had been very effective, so effective, that Jerry was inspired to enroll in night school to prepare himself for a promotion he was working toward. Within a year, he had been made lieutenant. As for his marriage, he and his wife eventually agreed to a separation, a decision Jerry came to see as the right next step in his life. I saw him recently; he told me that, looking back, he was actually grateful for the reassignment he'd had to deal with, "because otherwise I never would have made the step forward."

I want to emphasize that Jerry, who was initially skeptical of the group approach, benefited tremendously from it. It's like that with many officers. At first, the only "acceptable" way of sharing feelings or experiences they can envision is the time-honored, but potentially hazardous, one that comprises drinking alcohol with a buddy or two in a bar. Once they experience the benefits of working things out in a group setting, however, they tend to see these sessions as positive opportunities for growth and change, and are glad to have taken part.

(A number of activities designed for facilitation of group officer sessions appear in Chapter Ten of this book.)

# CHAPTER EIGHT

## Family Ties

*Love may be blind, but marriage*
*is the real eye-opener.*
—Unknown

A s we have seen, the occupational stressors associated with police work can be intense. They have been the subject of extensive academic research and, in my own case, a great deal of personal experience interacting with officers on the front lines, in the precinct, out on patrol, and in a counseling setting. This combination of scholarly evaluation and first-hand observation suggests to me two critical points that are important to the families of active officers, and especially to their spouses or partners.

First, there are definite work-related risk areas that can lead to various levels of dysfunction in the marriages and long-term relationships of police officers (Moore, 2004). It is essential that both officers and their partners identify what these risk areas are so they can be evaluated and discussed openly with the goal of supporting the relationship over time. In this chapter, I'll identify four such areas.

The second critical point follows directly from the first, because it concerns the spouse or partner of the officer. Very often, the domestic partners of police officers do not take advantage of the major role they can play in supporting a spouse's well-being and their own relationship's viability. The message for the spouse on this issue is a pretty simple one: *if you know there's a problem, DO something about it.* If you notice a member of your family is exhibiting signs of significant unresolved occupational stress—such as those outlined in the table below—you should encourage your partner to seek outside help, so that he or she can develop some effective coping strategies. If no help is sought, and your partner's "danger signs" stay the same or intensify, you should redouble your efforts to find some way to get your loved one into counseling, up to and including enlisting the help of other family members who can tactfully "double team" your life partner. One way or another, someone, some-how, has to cajole this person into talking to someone who can help.

*"That's Not Like Him/Her" — Possible Danger Signs of Unresolved Occupational Stress for Police Officers*

- Apparently disproportionate sadness
- Distraction
- Lack of focus
- Daydreaming
- Frequent mood changes
- Apparently disproportionate anger
- Memory lapses
- Explosive outbursts
- Constant complaining
- Increased dependence on alcohol or other substances

*continued on next page...*

*...continued from previous page*

- Diminished attention to detail
- Cynical or hostile remarks
- Overly critical of others
- Insubordinate to supervisors
- Downward changes in job productivity
- Withdrawn (when this was not part of behavior before stress)
- Increased self-criticism
- Generally negative disposition
- Impulsive actions

Now, let's look at the risk areas that may be worth discussing proactively with your spouse or life partner, whether or not you are currently experiencing problems in that area right now.

### Risk Area #1: Communication Shutdown

In an attempt to protect a spouse or life partner from the negativity, trauma, and degradation that is so commonly experienced as a daily reality of police work, some officers make the voluntary decision not to discuss any aspect of their working life while at home. Unfortunately, this lack of communication can lead to dysfunction for the couple, and there may be a feeling of "growing apart." An officer's inability or unwillingness to communicate about what he or she has actually experienced on the job can lead to instability and dissatisfaction in the couple's marriage. The simple act of discussing how one's day went, difficult though that act may sometimes be, turns out to be a significant shield against communication problems in the relationship. There are a number of communication tools that can help couples overcome the unhealthy "shutdown" pattern that undermines and endangers too many officer relationships; for more information on these tools, please visit www.drdebimoore.org.

### Risk Area #2: Domestic Absences

Many police families and relationships come under severe stress because the often-unpredictable schedule and long hours of the job ends up eating away at "family time." The police family may end up participating in many family-oriented activities without the spouse. This is a major problem, one that is often compounded by the

typical police department's rigid, quasi-military structure when it comes to setting up schedules for officers,
and by a working culture that does not always reward
flexibility and innovation. There are, unfortunately, not
likely to be any easy answers here. Beyond a willingness
to discuss the problem openly, accept the best intentions
of one's partner, and work together creatively to make
the most of "alternate" family times such as The Day After Christmas, this is one of those areas where the couple
may simply need to learn to adapt. To learn more about
adapting successfully as a family to the significant challenges of an active-duty police officer's work schedule,
feel free to reach out to me via www.drdebimoore.org.

## Risk Area #3: Assignments
## That Demand too Much, for too Long

It is one of the great ironies of police work that those
who take on certain particularly high-risk assignments
very often do not know when it is time for them to request a transfer to move on to another kind of work. Re-
calling my own situation, one where I had come to self-
identify strongly as a patrol officer over a period of five
years, I remember that I, too, was reluctant to move on

to another area of the department where I could make a contribution. My commanding officer pushed me to do so, however, and he was absolutely right. Many officers need a push like that. I'm thinking of those officers who come to identify strongly, as I did, with the work they do in areas such as narcotics enforcement, patrol duty, any kind of police work that routinely demands more or less permanent pattern of night shifts, or any assignment that routinely requires more than fifty hours a week. By "routinely," I mean week in and week out, for a number of years. I call these kinds of work arrangements "high-risk" assignments for a very good reason: academic research indicates that when assignments such as these become part of the officer's formal or informal job description, the officer is at an elevated risk to engage in some form of domestic violence. Obviously, that cycle must be avoided, even if an officer self-identifies strongly with a certain line of work. The negative cycle we are talking about here is debilitating and destructive to both the family and the officer, and there is simply no justification for perpetuating it. Some police departments have finally become more aware of the grave dangers of exposing officers to assignments that demand too much of them, for too long. These departments have taken a more responsible approach when it comes to determining who should receive these high-risk assignments, and for how long. Other departments, unfortunately, have yet to catch up to the research. If you are the spouse or partner of someone who has been in a high-risk assignment for an extended period, it is important you raise the subject of requesting a new assignment, even if your partner says he or she is happy with the current job. For more on the important subject of career growth and change for officers, contact me via www.drdebimoore.org.

### Risk Area #4: LGBT Issues

One of the last remaining areas where overt discrimination is still tolerated, and occasionally even encouraged, in many contemporary police departments is a broad prevailing bias against officers from the LGBT (lesbian, gay, bisexual, or transgender) community. This is an issue that directly or indirectly affects the families of a *majority* of officers, not just those who consider themselves members of this community, because the odds that any given officer is related to someone who does belong to this community is quite high. In 2010, the National Survey of Sexual Health and Behavior interviewed nearly 6,000 people nationwide between the ages of 14 and 94 found that seven percent of women and eight percent of men self-identified as gay, lesbian or bisexual; the numbers in metropolitan areas, such as greater New York City, are certainly higher than that. The stressors faced by LGBT police officers and their partners/spouses can be particularly difficult, in part because identifying openly as LGBT remains taboo in some circles. For help in providing individual support to these officers, contact me via www.drdebimoore.org.

# CHAPTER NINE

# The Leadership Imperative

> *"It is a curious thing, Harry, but perhaps those who
> are best suited to power are those who have never
> sought it. Those who, like you, have leadership thrust
> upon them, and take up the mantle because they must,
> and find to their own surprise that they wear it well."*
> —J.K. ROWLING, *Harry Potter
> and the Deathly Hallows* (2007)

n this next part of the book, we will look at the stressors—and opportunities—unique to those who aspire
to leadership positions within a police department.

## Leadership Stress

To the long list of stressors we have already identified, we can add the stress of fulfilling a leadership role within a police department. If you happen to be among those who believe you are not "cut out" for a leadership role, I urge you to read this part of the book particularly carefully. It is just possible that, a few years down the line, your initial reluctance to assume this role may end up being something you look back and laugh about. That was how it was for me. I certainly never expected to assume a leadership role within the New York City Police Department when I first enrolled at the Academy.

Serving as a leader in this setting can be an extremely stressful experience for anyone, particularly those who have not been prepared to take on this difficult and constantly changing role. In this part of the book, we will look at strategies for organizational development as well as resources for the support of current and emerging leadership within the department.

It is important to note first that the job of being a leader here is very different from the job of being a leader within a civilian setting (such as in a for-profit company). A leader within a police department supervises within a quasi-military environment, and must deal with a hierarchical structure that presents special challenges and opportunities. Very often, the rigid, unyielding structure within which these leaders work is a source of stress in and of itself, because the task of supporting subordinates and getting them what they need is often daunting in such an environment. The leaders themselves frequently deal with problems of long-term unmet needs in precisely the same areas—such as career assignments, personality conflicts, or scheduling—that their subordinates are asking them about. The result, all too often, is a variety of cynicism that can come to seem "part of the territory."

Cynicism is the assumption that life is difficult, that the game is usually fixed, that nothing ever changes much, and that people are motivated by their self- purposes. This attitude, which frequently results in self-fulfilling prophecies, can become a way of life if we're not careful. It is the opposite of leadership. It is not accepted as "part of the territory" for a true leader in a police environment ... or at least it does not have to be. To change this attitude of cynicism, or prevent it from arising in the first place, requires sustained, formal leadership training. This training, however, is something that most people promoted to leadership positions within police departments never receive. And that's usually what allows cynicism to creep in.

## Good Officer, Good Sergeant

*"If we listened to our intellect we'd never have a love affair. We'd never have a friendship. We'd never go in business because we'd be cynical: "It's gonna go wrong." Or "She's going to hurt me." Or, "I've had a couple of bad love affairs, so therefore . . ." Well, that's nonsense. You're going to miss life. You've got to jump off the cliff all the time and build your wings on the way down."*

—RAY BRADBURY

This part of the book is about making sure good officers don't become cynical leaders.

The critical point at which cynicism is likely to set in among leaders within a police department lies somewhere within the difficult transition from rank-and-file officer to sergeant, which is the first step on the leadership ladder. It is in this transition, in my experience, that the officer's potential is either awakened in a positive and constructive way, or neglected in a way that leads to a cynical outlook—and severely limits the new sergeant's potential to contribute.

In the pages that follow, I'll offer some resources designed especially for "incoming" sergeants, resources that can, if shared with compassion and a willingness to listen, protect both the individual and the organization from creeping cynicism during a period where both are particularly vulnerable to it.

What I'm about to share should, I believe, be required reading **and re-reading** for anyone within a police department who is being considered for promotion to the rank of sergeant. I strongly recommend all new and incoming sergeants carefully read what follows, and gather a facilitated group to discuss its application to their own lives, at least every three months during their first year in the new rank (see also the LEADERSHIP activities for Lay Peer Facilitators that appear in Chapter Ten of this book).

## What Is A Sergeant?

*Be a yardstick of quality. Some people aren't used
to an environment where excellence is expected.*

—STEVE JOBS

Congratulations. You are, or are about to become, a police sergeant. What is that, exactly?

Most civilians imagine they know exactly what a police sergeant does. How could they not know? They've been watching gruff but loveable police sergeants bark out instructions, keep headstrong rookies in line, and threaten bad guys for most of their lives—while watching television shows, of course!

In the real world, the role of the sergeant is defined, not by a scriptwriter, but by the law enforcement organization to whom he or she reports. There may or may not be a formal job description—and when there isn't, that's a danger sign, a sign there is still work to be done on behalf of the department.

Something that may be overlooked in the sergeant's job description is the importance of his or her organizational role. Sergeants are the links between front-line officers and senior management. They are the front-line supervisors upon whom the entire chain of command depends.

Whether or not you are guided by a job description, you will eventually find the role of the sergeant is defined by many factors that cannot be reflected in a brief written summary of the job: organizational culture (broadly understood by officers and supervisors alike as "the way we do things around here"), values (the shared moral standards that make culture possible), formal policies and rules, unwritten "ground rules," and the expectations, stated and unstated, of supervisors, other members of the department, members of the public, and members of the media, to name just a few.

These are just some of the many constituencies and intangible forces likely to have some kind of influence on your answer to the question "What is a sergeant?" The problem arises once you realize these different forces may well be in conflict. You and your commanding officer must be in full agreement about what is and isn't part of your role. That means you need agreement on what your job actually entails. And that means you both need to review the job description. When in doubt, the job description must be the "compass point" that allows you and your commanding officer to be in alignment about what you should be doing, why you should be doing it, and (perhaps just as important) what you should not be doing.

This is why my very first piece of advice to new and incoming sergeants is quite simple: **study your written job description carefully, and then go out to lunch with your supervisor so that the two of you can discuss it in depth, without interruption.** Is it accurate? Is it up-to-date? Is your commanding officer in agreement about what it lays out? Are *you* in agreement with what it lays out?

**If you do not have a formal written job description, or you have one that you know your commanding officer considers deficient, flawed, or incomplete, then your job is a little bit different.** In this case, what I want you to do is write your own draft of your ideal job description (don't ask for permission to do this, just do it) then ask your commanding officer to go out to lunch with you in order to review and offer constructive criticism about what you have written. In issuing this invitation, it's important that you let your commanding officer know that you are looking for guidance and support so you can be absolutely certain about what is and isn't expected of you. Explain that you have no "pride of ownership" in anything you have written, and that the most successful outcome from your perspective is one where your commanding officer scribbles all over the sheet you have written and gives you lots of corrections (if it helps to show your commanding officer this part of the book, then by all means do so).

In either of these situations, it is perfectly acceptable for your commanding officer to review the job description with you during a private meeting, without going out to lunch. I am suggesting the route of at least making a request for a lunch date for two reasons: first, because it is a good opportunity to escape the distractions of the precinct, and second, because it will probably remind your commanding officer of the vital importance of occasional one-on-one meetings with sergeants, and with you in particular.

The important thing is the job description be finalized, and both you and your commanding officer agree on its particulars. When the department does not delineate the sergeant's role explicitly, or the written description of the role is no longer relevant to the world in which the sergeant must operate, there is no way for the sergeant and the commanding officer to be in alignment about the objectives and values that will guide the sergeant's work. The result, all too often, is poor communication between the individuals involved, a lack of personal job satisfaction for the sergeant, and a culture of mediocrity for the organization as a whole. Mediocrity is not where we want to go. We always want to be headed for excellence. And that, I hope, is the definition of "sergeant" that you and your commanding officer will decide upon together, and return to regularly: someone who is dedicated to excellence in law enforcement.

## A Sample Job Description

*There are few, if any, jobs in which ability alone
is sufficient. Needed, also, are loyalty, sincerity,
enthusiasm and team play.*
—WILLIAM B. GIVEN, JR.

Below is a job description for a sergeant's position, adapted from descriptions circulated by several police departments. If you wish, you may use it as a model. As a general rule, it is better for you and your commanding office to agree on a detailed job description, such as this one, than on one that is so brief as to be useless; such as "Supervise, support, and schedule officers; other duties as required."

---

## JOB TITLE

Police Sergeant

## OVERVIEW

Protects public safety at a high level of managerial excellence and integrity.

## ESSENTIAL DUTIES

- Serves and protects the public by performing a variety of routine and complex public safety work in the administration and execution of police patrol, investigation, traffic regulation, and related law enforcement activities.

- Normally works under the general supervision of Police Lieutenant.

- Exercises general supervision over police officers and other staff, as assigned.

- Supervises police officers and other assigned staff in their duties.

- Supervises the scheduling and coordinating of shift activities.

- Reviews a variety of police-related reports prepared by subordinate officers and others.

- Evaluates officers' arrests based on circumstances and evidence to determine whether subject should be temporarily detained or placed in jail.

- Makes day-to-day police assignments as required by the needs of the service.

- Makes plans about individual tactical matters such as equipment to be used for particular operations or the detailed plans required for an investigation.

- Develops new approaches to investigative challenges.

- Advises supervisors in deployment of personnel during emergency responses.

- Maintains contact with all police personnel to coordinate investigation activities, provide mutual assistance during emergency situations, and provide general information about Department activities.

- Maintains contact with general public, court officials, and other city officials in the performance of police activities, as assigned.

- Conducts periodic performance evaluation and planning sessions for assigned personnel.

- Counsels assigned personnel on job performance, stress management, and disciplinary matters.

- Seeks and provides support for officers as individual circumstances warrant.

- Works uniformed shifts as required and supervises the performance of security patrols, traffic control, investigation and first aid at accident scenes, detection, investigation and arrest of persons involved in crimes or misconduct.

- Supervises police officers on patrol as they patrol streets, parks, commercial areas, and residential areas to preserve the peace and enforce the law, control vehicular traffic, prevent and/or detect and investigate misconduct involving misdemeanors, felonies, and other law violations.

- Maintains normal availability by radio, telephone, or text message for consultation on major emergencies.

- Carries out duties in conformance with federal, state, county, and city laws and ordinances.

- Supervises vehicular accidents.

- Prepares a variety of reports and records regarding officer's daily performance.

- Coordinates and supervises the training, assignment, support, and career development of subordinate police officers.

- Coordinates activities with supervisors or other city departments; exchanges information with officers in other law enforcement agencies; obtains advice from municipal officials regarding cases, policies, and procedures.

- Performs various tasks requiring good physical condition, as required.

- Communicates effectively, both orally and in writing.

- Establishes and maintains effective working relationships with subordinates, peers, supervisors, and the general public.

- Follows and gives clear verbal and written instructions.

- Exercises sound judgment in evaluating situations, making decisions, and seeking guidance from others.

- Establishes and maintains effective working relationships with members of the general public, fellow employees, city officials, and others.

- Note: Attendance at work is an essential function of this position. Sergeants are required to perform shift work that includes days, evenings, nights, weekends, and holidays.

## NON-ESSENTIAL DUTIES

- Analyzes and recommends improvements to equipment and facilities as needed.

- Reviews, evaluates, and develops specific programs in support of the identified requirements of members of the department.

- Suggests revisions to department policies and procedures.

- Maintains liaison with community groups.

- Note: The duties listed above are intended only as illustrations of the various types of work that may be performed. The omission of specific statements of duties does not exclude them from the position if the work is similar, related, or a logical assignment within the position.

## Cultural Responsibilities

In order to help maintain a Departmental culture of excellence, the sergeant is also expected to model, support, and defend internal values of:

- Excellence

- Integrity, including but not limited to respect for the letter and spirit of the law

- Helpfulness

- Proactivity

- Mutual support and understanding in times of stress

- A willingness to ask for, give and receive support

- Support for a zero-tolerance policy concerning drug abuse.

It is worth noting, before we move on, that many police departments have outdated job descriptions that completely ignore important duties related to supporting fellow officers who ask for help in dealing with stress, and being able to ask for such help yourself. This omission alone is sufficient reason to ask for a meeting with your commanding officer to discuss how your job description can best be brought up to date.

## The Leadership Imperative

*Destiny is what you are supposed to do in life. Fate is what kicks you in the pants to make you do it.*
—Henry Miller

Suppose you go to the trouble of reviewing (or creating) the job description for sergeant ... and you still find yourself wondering whether you're actually up for the job?

Once you learn that you are, or are soon to become, a sergeant within your department, you are about to experience a major cultural and career shift. Feelings of uncertainty, and even a desire to withdraw from the process, are not uncommon. That you may initially feel resistant to that shift is natural enough. You may even be willing to share with your commanding officer the misgivings you may have concerning feelings you are not up to the demands of the new job. Before you take this step (which in and of itself is a healthy one), my advice is that you take a good, long look at whether or not you are simply falling back on what is most familiar. That's what I did when my own commanding officer suggested that I move off patrol duty and take on a counseling role. I was resistant to his suggestion. Today I'm glad I listened to him and overcame that resistance.

I would also advise you to at least consider the possibility this new role is indeed one you are supposed to play, and accept the prospect your commanding officer's decision to move you into the ranks of management may indeed be based on his or her seeing something in you that you have overlooked. In short, I am asking you to accept the possibility that this is the right next step for you, and consider it closely before rejecting it outright. I say this because there is a likely possibility that the transition you are being asked to make may well be the most important one of your career, difficult as it may seem in the moment. Very often in life, others see potential in us we never noticed in ourselves. Very often in life, we are presented with challenges that look like they are too big for us, challenges that turn out to be the perfect next step. Very often in life, we need a kick in the pants.

I call this kick in the pants toward taking a challenging "right next step" *The Leadership Imperative*. It can take many different forms. There may be more than one of these in a career. For me, *The Leadership Imperative* took the form of a transition into a counseling role for which I was not enthusiastic, and (so I thought) not prepared. As it turned out, I was more prepared than I realized. This is often how it is with officers who turn into great sergeants.

For officers who have put in five or more years on patrol (a common career profile among those asked to make the transition to sergeant) the moment of *The Leadership Imperative* is a moment of choice. It is a particularly critical choice for you, your family, and the community you serve. If you are fortunate, this moment can be the "kick in the pants" that keeps you from turning into a cynical officer.

Many of us, after we have spent a certain amount of time out on the street, run the risk of beginning a cycle of dissatisfaction, overload, and disengagement as a result of that long tour of duty. Here's the challenge: we may not be able to spot that cycle when it first emerges, simply because we have become too used to the routine and camaraderie of patrol duty, and perhaps also because we have grown used to the identity of being an officer who works out on patrol.

Most people are not used to going beyond their own comfort zones and challenging their own long-established roles and identities, and it may take an "intervention" from someone else, someone with enough insight and experience to realize that we need a change, to get us to set out on a new course, accept a little uncertainty, and embrace the reality that a change is what we need in order to grow as law enforcement professionals, and as people. That is certainly how it was with me. Had I stayed out on the street—which is what I thought I wanted at the time—I would have missed an extremely important opportunity for personal and professional development. I suspect you may find yourself in a similar position at some point. Perhaps this book can serve as the signpost that helps you to identify the right next step in your career.

William Jennings Bryan once said, "Destiny is not a

matter of chance; it is a matter of choice. It is not a thing to be waited for, it is a thing to be achieved." I believe *The Leadership Imperative* is that choice, and for most police officers who encounter it, it takes the form of a choice about whether or not to move out of their comfort zone and take on the challenge of a new identity. Not everyone, of course, is cut out to be a leader. But it is also possible that *you* are cut out for this role.

How will you *know for sure* whether or not you are cut out to be a leader within your department? That's what we'll be examining next.

### "Am I Cut Out for This?"

*Understand the law, the profession and*
*our constitution so you understand your*
*responsibility to the people and the trust you are*
*granted—and to stay true to it.*
—SHERIFF DAVE BROWN

There are eleven tested, proven principles of great leaders. If you are willing to adopt these principles and live by them, you can become a good—perhaps even a great—leader. Notice that you do not have to be living by all eleven principles *right now* in order to be a good leader in a police department. If you aspire toward them, then make steady progress you will reach your goal. If you can do that, then you can rest assured that you are in fact "cut out for this."

The eleven principles of leadership are:

1. Know yourself and seek self-improvement.
2. Be technically and tactically proficient.
3. Seek responsibility, and take responsibility for your actions.
4. Make sound and timely decisions.
5. Set the example.
6. Know your officers and look out for their well-being.
7. Keep your subordinates informed.
8. Develop a sense of responsibility in your subordinates.
9. Ensure the task is understood, supervised, and accomplished.
10. Build the team.
11. Employ your unit in accordance with its capabilities.

You might be interested in the origin of the eleven principles I've just shared with you. They are not my invention. They are adapted from the U.S. Army's classic *Eleven Principles of Army Leadership* (1983), first developed as part of a 1948 leadership study whose aim was to determine what the most effective leaders in the U.S. Army had in common. I believe they still stand as letter-perfect enunciations of the fundamental objectives of effective leadership in all fields: military, police, civilian, and any other field you can come up with in which one individual must lead a group. I've been sharing this summary of principles with emerging and established leaders in metropolitan police departments for years, and have never received any "push back" concerning the accuracy or validity of the eleven principles.

For the record, the only change I have made in the wording of these eleven principles, in order to adapt them to the world of policing, appears in Principle 6, which originally read, "Know your soldiers and look out for their well-being." I have changed the word "soldiers" to "officers." Other than that, the timeless principles I have laid out above are, word-for-word, the same ones that have stood for more than half a century as the official leadership doctrine of the U.S. Army.

**Use these principles to assess yourself and develop an action plan to awaken and/or improve your own ability to lead!**

I believe that effective leaders are not born, but self-made. Successful leaders only *become* successful by internalizing the principles of effective leadership, and constantly refining and improving their own leadership skill set. The more you practice leadership, the better you will be at it, and the more effective you will be when officers and members of the public look to you for leadership.

Let's look at each of the eleven leadership principles in depth. I have freely adapted the summaries that follow from the classic Army text, so as to make the descriptions relevant to prospective leaders who will operate in a law enforcement environment. As you consider each of these principles, think about all the ways that doing a better job of living that principle, day in and day out, could improve your department and enable it to more effectively fulfill its mission of helping the members of the community you are sworn to serve and protect. Think, too, about how building each of these principles into your daily life could improve the safety and quality of life of the community in which you live. Last, but not least, as you peruse this list, ask yourself whether you feel you could live these principles at least as well as the people in leadership positions whom you have encountered in your own career. Most officers, after all, live and work in a world in which there are too many managers and not enough true leaders. If, after reading what follows, you feel, deep down inside, that you could improve that ratio … you should consider accepting the challenge of *The Leadership Imperative*.

**1. Know yourself and seek self-improvement.** This means you commit to analyzing yourself objectively to determine both your strong and weak points. Knowing yourself allows you to take advantage of your strengths and work steadily to overcome your weaknesses. Seeking self-improvement means continually developing your strengths and working on minimizing or perhaps even eliminating your weaknesses. This will increase your competence, your own self-confidence, and the level of confidence that your officers have in your ability to train, develop, and lead them.

**2. Be technically and tactically proficient.** This means you commit to learning, relearning, and practicing what is necessary to accomplish all the tasks for which you are responsible in executing your mission. As a leader, you are expected to know what the right tools are and how to use them; this is technical proficiency. You are also expected to know what specific actions will be most likely to bring about the attainment of your goals and the department's goals, and be comfortable taking those actions; this is tactical proficiency. In addition, you are ultimately responsible for ensuring that your people are properly trained for their jobs.

**3. Seek responsibility and take responsibility for your actions.** Leading always involves responsibility. Of course, you will want subordinates who can handle responsibility and help you perform your mission. Similarly, your commanding officers want you to take the initiative within their stated intent. When you see a problem, or see something that needs to be fixed, do not wait for your leader to tell you to act. The example you set, whether positive or negative, will have an effect on those officers who report to you. Your objective should be to build trust between you and your leaders, and between you and those you lead, by actively seeking and accepting responsibility.

**4. Make sound and timely decisions.** This means you must be able to assess situations rapidly and make good choices about the situations you face. If you delay or try to avoid making a decision, you may cause unnecessary problems (up to and perhaps including problems that cause loss of life) and you may undermine the department's goal of serving and protecting the public. Indecisive leaders create hesitancy, loss of confidence, and confusion. Even in the most trying conditions, you must be able to anticipate, reason, and quickly decide what actions to take.

**5. Set the example.** Your people want and need you to be a role model. This is a heavy responsibility, but a leader has no choice. No aspect of leadership is more powerful than this aspect of setting the right example. If you expect courage, competence, candor, commitment, and integrity from your officers, you must demonstrate these qualities to them. Your officers will emulate your behavior. You must set high, but attainable, standards.

**6. Know your officers and look out for their well-being.** You must know and care for your people. It is not enough to know their names. You need to understand "what makes them tick," what is important to them. You need to commit time and effort listening to and learning about your subordinates. Become friendly (but not over-familiar) with them; be approachable. Never reprimand officers in public. Offer ample, credible praise in public. Help your officers get needed support from available personal services or agencies.

**7. Keep your subordinates informed.** Explain what tasks are required and, if applicable, why they are required. Be alert to the spread of rumors; replace rumors with the truth whenever it is feasible to do so. Keep your officers updated on command-level and department procedures and policies.

**8. Develop a sense of responsibility in your subordinates.** Your officers will feel a sense of pride and responsibility when they successfully accomplish a new task you have given them. Strategically sound delegation indicates that you trust your officers; it also makes it more likely they will want even more responsibility. Remember that, as a leader, you are a teacher, and are responsible for developing your officers.

**9. Ensure the task is understood, supervised, and accomplished.** This means making sure your officers understand what is expected of them. They need to know what you want accomplished, and in what specific way it should be accomplished. They need to know what you want done, what is standard operating procedure in carrying it out, and when you want it completed. Supervising lets you know whether your officers actually understand your orders. It also shows your interest in them—and in mission accomplishment. Remember always that you must strive to strike a balance: Over supervision causes resentment, while under supervision causes frustration.

**10. Build the team.** You must develop a team spirit in your officers that motivates them to go willingly and confidently into situations that might be dangerous or even fatal. To do this, they need confidence in your ability to lead them, and in their own abilities to perform as members of the team. You must train and cross-train your officers until they are confident in the technical and tactical abilities of the team as a whole. Your unit only becomes a team when your officers trust and respect you, and each other, as trained professionals. Each individual must see and appreciate the importance of his or her personal contributions.

**11. Employ your unit in accordance with its capabilities.** This means you must be sure that tasks assigned to officers are reasonable. Assign tasks equitably and fairly among your officers. Analyze all assigned tasks;

use your available resources to the fullest before requesting assistance. In particular, constantly evaluate and re-
evaluate your training. Do your best to incorporate more
innovative and effective training techniques; take every
opportunity to re-examine and revise the conditions under which the training is being conducted. Set assignments that are challenging, but attainable; do not lower
standards simply because your unit has not yet met them.

**Those are the Army's eleven classic leadership prin-
ciples.** If I had to add a twelfth, it would probably involve giving your subordinates appropriate support in
dealing with stress (see specifically chapters eight and
ten of this book), being able to talk with them one-on-
one about their own personal experiences with stress,
and providing them with appropriate second chances
after they have developed coping strategies for managing that stress. Do not let a bad day, a bad week, or even
a bad couple of months, cloud your judgment about an
officer's ability to bounce back and make a contribution.
Everyone drops the ball from time to time, and most of
us are unfortunate enough, at some point or another in
our careers, to drop the ball when a game is on the line.
Give your officer a chance to rebound. Remember Mi-

chael Jordan's wise words: "I've missed more than 9000 shots in my career. I've lost almost 300 games. 26 times, I've been trusted to take the game winning shot and missed. I've failed over and over and over again in my life. And that is why I succeed."

The reality is, if you are an effective patrol officer, you already play a leadership role in the larger community ... and for many (but not all) officers, the transition to internal leadership is a natural extension of an already existing leadership skill set. If you feel, having read what I have shared with you here, you are one of those officers, my message to you is simple and direct: **accept the challenge of *The Leadership Imperative* ... and get ready for the ride of your life!**

> *The police are the public and the public are the police; the police being only members of the public who are paid to give full time attention to duties which are incumbent on every citizen in the interests of community welfare and existence.*
> —ROBERT PEEL

## 25 Common Mistakes Made by New Supervisors

1. Making changes for the sake of change

2. Without consultation, ordering major revisions in policies concerning discipline or procedure

3. Unable to listen/effectively interact with members of the public

4. Failing to take charge of the department

5. Ignoring existing administrative procedures

6. Trying to be "one of the guys"

7. Doing the work of subordinates

8. Failing to delegate

9. Giving subordinates no positive reinforcement

10. Applying inconsistent problem-solving standards (usually indicates a sign of a lack of core values. Core values should always drive problem-solving and decision-making)

11. Failing to solicit input from subordinates

12. Failing to listen to subordinates

13. Showing favoritism among subordinates

14. Failing to make timely decisions

15. Not addressing problems raised by subordinates

16. Failing to utilize time effectively

17. Failing to motivate subordinates

18. Poor written and/or verbal communication skills (and/or failure to delegate to someone who does have these skills)

19. Not understanding contents/requirements of paperwork

20. Failure to foster positive interdepartmental relations

21. Failure to document positive and negative activities of subordinates

22. Offering only negative feedback and/or criticizing an officer in public

23. Failing to deal with problems promptly

24. Unwilling to seek advice from own supervisor

25. Lacking basic knowledge of labor laws, contracts, and/or personnel procedures

## 25 Traits of Excellent Supervisors

1. Sets clear goals

2. Is fair

3. Gives positive reinforcement

4. Stays up-to-date and is knowledgeable

5. Is genuinely interested in subordinates on a personal level

6. Respects subordinates

7. Is honest

8. Sets the example

9. Has patience

10. Is decisive

11. Knows leadership is about teaching

12. Backs the decisions of subordinates to whom he/she has delegated authority; does not play "Monday Morning Quarterback"

13. Is a good listener

14. Delegates strategically

15. Is accessible

16. Good written communication skills

17. Good oral communication skills

18. Accountable; assumes personal responsibility

19. Is consistent

20. Is willing to help

21. Takes command

22. Doesn't hold grudges

23. Shows genuine enthusiasm for his/her work

24. Gives constructive feedback

25. Strikes the right balance; does not undermanage or over manage

# CHAPTER TEN

# Tools And Resources For Peer Counselors

*When our communication supports*

*compassionate giving and receiving, happiness*

*replaces violence and grieving.*

—MARSHALL ROSENBERG

**W**hat follows in this section are the most effective tools, resources and exercises I have developed over the years in support of police well-being. They are intended for use by the practitioner or facilitator who is a peer of an officer, or group of officers, and who takes on the role of "helper of the helpers." Note that most of these activities unfold in a group setting, which makes the third element, *Guidelines for Facilitators*, particularly important. Also worth noting, depending on the needs of your department these exercises can be done in any order and may vary slightly.

The resources you will find in this chapter are as follows:

I.   Overview: The Helpers Who
     Help The Helpers
II.  Types of Therapy
III. Guidelines for Facilitators
IV.  Activity: "Our Accomplishments"
V.   Activity: "Organizational Path"
VI.  Activity: "Dealing with Organizational Stress"
VII. Activity: "Understanding and
     Managing Blind Rage"
VIII. Activity: "Outstanding Qualities"
IX.  Activity: "Letting Go of Cynicism"
X.   Activity: "Stress Management"

## I. Overview: The Helpers Who Help The Helpers

*The dispensable trappings of dogma may*
*determine what a therapist thinks he is doing,*
*what he talks about when he talks about therapy,*
*but the agent of change is who he is.*
—THOMAS LEWIS

Those of us who are fortunate enough to provide help to officers who are dealing with stress may deliver help in a number of different ways. We may obtain our training by pursuing one or more of a large number of professional disciplines. A brief summary of the major categories of "helpers who help the helpers" follows.

At the end, following the list of formally accredited professionals, I have added a special entry for the helper who may lack professional status ... but who may be able to provide important support, guidance, and insight to officers who find themselves without access to professional, therapeutic treatment. (This all-too-common scenario of an officer having no access to a credentialed therapist who is qualified to address the special requirements of police can exist for any number of reasons, including the very likely one that the department is under-budgeted and under-resourced.)

*Psychiatrists.* These are physicians (MDs) who have completed three years in psychiatric residency following the successful completion of medical school. Psychiatrists can legally prescribe medication.

*Psychologists.* Not to be confused with psychiatrists. They hold a medical degree and a Ph. D. or Psy.D. degree in counseling, or an Ed. D. in counseling or educational psychology. Their training includes four years of graduate course work and a dissertation, a year of postdoctoral work, supervised clinical experience, and preparation for passing a written exam for licensure. At a somewhat lower degree of credential are Master level psychologists, who complete two years of graduate work, write and defend a thesis, and prepare for a similar written examination that establishes licensure.

*Clinical Social Workers.* These are therapists who possess a license or certification in social work. They have completed two years of academic work, a thesis project, and supervised clinical experience. They are also required to complete a written examination.

*Mental Health Counselors.* These therapists have a Ph. D. or Masters degree in counseling or a related mental health field. Some, but not all, states require them to be licensed. Mental Health Counselors have completed

3000 hours of supervised clinical work and passed a national written exam.

*Marriage and Family Therapists.* These therapists hold a doctorate or a Masters degree in Marriage and Family Therapy or a related mental health field. They have completed a specialized course of training and supervised experience in marriage and family therapy. Clinical members of the American Association of Marriage and Family Therapists complete an additional two years of postgraduate training.

*Psychoanalysts.* These therapists specialize in mental health and have completed postgraduate training in some form of psychoanalytic theory. Classical psychoanalytical theories include those of the two most famous researchers in this field, Sigmund Freud and Carl Jung, but in the century that has passed since their initial breakthroughs, many other schools have emerged.

*Lay Peer Facilitator.* This person is not a therapist, but brings direct personal experience from the realm of police work to the process of creating positive coping strategies for dealing with stress. A lay peer facilitator can augment or initiate a process that leads to formal therapy delivered by one or more of the caregivers listed above.

## The Helpers Who Help The Helpers

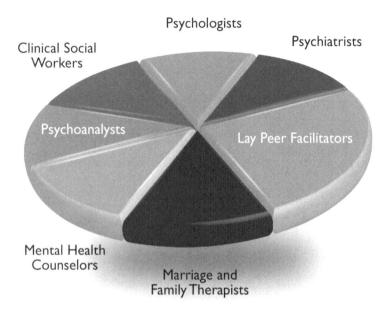

## II. Types Of Therapy

*I know a lot of people think therapy is about sitting*
*around staring at your own navel—but it's staring*
*at your own navel with a goal. And the goal is to*
*one day see the world in a better way and treat your*
*loved ones with more kindness and have more to give.*

—HUGH LAURIE

"Helpers of the helpers" use a variety of intervention
tools to help officers learn to deal constructively with

stress and create positive coping strategies. Listed below are some of the most common approaches.

*Individual Therapy.* This involves one-on-one interaction between a formally credentialed therapist and a client (Lay Peer Facilitators cannot deliver this method because they are not therapists). Individual therapy involves sessions that are scheduled for at least once a week and usually last around fifty minutes. Individual therapy works best for people who are not comfortable in a group setting, or whose specific problems do not lend themselves to group discussions.

*Couple Therapy.* This is effective for situations where two people in a committed relationship are experiencing difficulties. Couple therapy is also used in premarital and divorce settings. In couple therapy, each person in the relationship has the opportunity to express his or her feelings and point of view, with the therapist acting as a neutral sounding board for addressing conflicts, complaints, and other challenges. Couple therapy is meant to help partners identify underlying issues in the relationship, teach communication skills, and conflict resolution techniques.

*Family Therapy.* This type of therapy addresses not only problems that confront spouses or committed partners, but also problems that arise in relationships between parents (and/or step-parents) and children. Family counseling allows interaction among family members in a safe setting where they can express their feelings and explore family roles without the fear of ridicule or punishment.

*Group Therapy.* This kind of therapy offers a forum that allows participants to enhance interpersonal skills and learn to build a support network—at the same time they resolve individual emotional problems. In this format, group members share feelings, ideas, and problems with one another as well as with the therapist. These interactions often help participants become more aware of unproductive behavior patterns. Some groups are centered on specific issues or concerns (such as family issues or recovery). Group sessions generally take place once a week and last for between one and three hours.

*Lay Peer Facilitation.* This peer-driven, peer-led approach is typically modeled on group therapy, although, of course, the interactions led by a lay peer facilitator can't be considered "therapy" in the strict sense, because the person leading it has no formal degree. But then, the same can be said of group-driven support group encounters such as Alcoholics Anonymous and Overeaters Anonymous, and few would dispute these meetings can create solidarity, a shared commitment to positive change, and the ability to share "best practices." The idea is to facilitate—not lecture—the group's various experiences and suggestions relevant to the development of healing and coping strategies. In cases where the aim is to help police officers develop positive coping responses to stresses they face in daily life, I believe there are times when a well-prepared and empathetic peer without a degree is likely to be more helpful than a "qualified" therapist who is perceived as an outsider by the group. For an extensive collection of resources designed specifically for use by lay peers in group settings, see Chapter Ten.

## Types Of Therapy

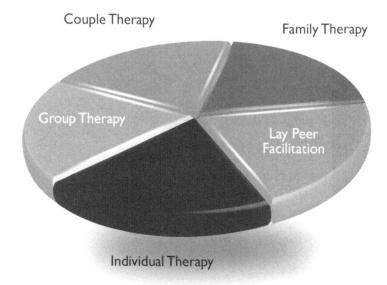

## What Makes a Great Lay Peer Facilitator?

You don't need an advanced degree to be a great lay peer facilitator who serves police officers. You do need to be someone who:

- Empathizes with the experiences of fellow officers as someone who has "been there"

- Is considerate of the feelings of others

- Looks at a situation, takes hold of it and starts a dialogue about possible solutions

- Lets others speak

- Finds ways to get reluctant participants to take part in group discussions

- Admits being wrong and takes steps to correct the mistake, whatever it may be

- Is not afraid to get involved

- Listens with an open mind

- Is prudent and tactful, yet also forceful and firm when that is appropriate

- Never quits on someone

- Never complains

- Is easy to interact with

- Is accurate

- Does not spread gossip

- Is thorough

- Is reliable

- Takes the initiative and kindles the interest and involvement of others

---

What's interesting to me is that these are also some of the qualities of a great leader!

## III. Guidelines For Facilitators

First and foremost, remember that your job is to help participants feel comfortable exploring internal issues, concerns, and problems they may have with the department. Your first priority then is to establish an agreement of confidentiality. This Agreement must be binding on all in attendance, and those who choose not to make this commitment must exclude themselves from the gathering. All those in attendance must feel free to express themselves without adverse career consequences. The obvious exceptions to the group agreement regarding confidentiality are illegal activities and behavior that is likely to harm oneself or others. Beyond those two basic guidelines, complete confidentiality is a precondition of taking part in the exercise. You may want to mention the ad tag line, "What happens in Vegas stays in Vegas." This remark will probably generate a laugh—an important rapport-building step in and of itself—and make the confidentiality point clear for each individual member of the group.

Your primary role is to promote exploration and discussion. That means you must lecture less and facilitate more. The physical layout of the room can help you keep lecturing to a minimum. Consider setting the chairs up in a U shape "horseshoe format." This will promote engagement and keep one person from dominating the group conversation. Always remember that your goal is to engage everyone in the process.

Invite diverse input. Keep in mind the individual viewpoints of the participants can often shed more light on what is happening in someone's life, and what the new possibilities are, than your opinion as facilitator. Encourage feedback by asking questions such as, "What did you think of what he/she just said?"

Let the group determine when a subject has been examined in enough detail. Share your own ideas for discussion only *after* the participants have shared their own thoughts and feelings.

When you pose a question, be prepared to "wait out" the silence that follows. Offer a prompt or suggested response only after a significant pause of, say, twenty seconds.

## IV. Activity: "Our Accomplishments"

The purpose of this group activity is to identify the accomplishments of officers in your department, many of which go unrecognized by the public, the media, and even an officer's own supervisor. In some cases, an officer may take his or her own accomplishments for granted!

Start by asking participants: *What contributions have officers of this department made to the residents of and visitors to this community?*

Possible response categories include, but are not limited to:

- Increased sense of community safety due to officer presence;
- Reduction of experiences of psychological and physical trauma in civilian population;
- Safer neighborhood environments have allowed adults, youth, children, and the elderly to live more fulfilling lives, thanks to a reduction in wor-

ry about being victimized by crime;

- Safer community environment for tourists to visit.

List these responses on a flip chart or other display tool. Then, when the topic has been explored fully, ask: *Despite our accomplishments, what issues are still present for us to work on?*

Possible response categories include, but are not limited to:

- Gaining public and media trust in police;
- Expanding public and media awareness of police contributions;
- High rates of stress for police and their families;
- Family issues such as lack of sufficient time at home;
- Relationship issues such as separation and divorce;
- Incidents of excessive use of force.

List these responses, too, on a flip chart or other display tool. Then, when the topic has been explored fully, **verbally summarize all the points you have written down.**

Then say something like: *Based on what we have seen*

so far, I think we can all agree the efforts of police officers have positively affected the lives of many, many people. The knowledge we have about the contributions we make to the community serve as the foundation of everything else we will do together to address the other issues we identified;

One of the things we see is that a lack of balance in one's home life expresses itself in a lack of balance on the job, and vice versa. The two areas inevitably affect one another;

Everything you share here today will help us make progress toward developing a more balanced, more supportive working environment ... which means a more balanced and happier life at home.

## V. Activity: "Organizational Path"

The purpose of this group activity is to challenge participants to explore where they want to be in the department, and brainstorm how to get there. It is common, particularly in large departments, for people to feel "trapped" or "stifled" by their career path, or by organizational demands and structure. This exercise strives to help people focus on the positive and chart a course that makes sense.

Start by saying, *Let's each look at our own personal ORGANIZATIONAL PATH. To do that, I want you to get ready to answer these questions. Don't worry, this is not a writing activity. There are no wrong answers.*

(Write or reveal these questions on a flipchart or display tool, then read them aloud:)

What is my current assignment?

_____

_____

How long have I been doing this assignment?

_____

_____

Am I happy with what I am currently doing?

_____

_____

Do I think I've been doing this assignment for too long?

_____

_____

If I had a choice, would I choose to work in this unit/department?

_____

_____

In the next two to five years, I anticipate that I will….

Now say, *Let's go around the room and see how each of you respond to each of these six questions.*

Discuss each person's (on-the-spot) responses to each of the questions. On questions that generate a "Yes" or "No" response, be prepared to ask, *Why do you say that?* or, *What makes you feel like that's the right answer?*

After each member of the group has contributed an answer, and you have elicited appropriate feedback from other members, say, *Now I would like you to take the time to write out some answers. Please break into groups of two and complete these worksheets.*

Complete these sentences in your own words.

1. Over the next two to five years, my career goal is to....

_____

_____

2. Something I have already done to make this happen is to....

_____

_____

2a. Answer only if you left 2 above blank, or wrote an answer like "Nothing." The main thing that has prevented me from getting more information about this and taking action is....

( ) Not really sure the unit is for me.

( ) Not sure I have the right credentials.

( ) Feel I have little or no chance of getting into this unit

( ) I heard that you "need to know someone" to get in there

Other:

_____

Something I am willing to make a personal commitment to do within the next 14 days to make this happen is....

_____

_____

Say: *Once you are done, swap your work with your partner, and after you've read what's there, offer the other person your own suggestions on how best to get where he or she wants to go; and*

*Once you are done, revise your worksheet to incorporate the feedback you receive from your partner.*

Pair up with anyone who is left without a partner for this process. Help him or her to create positive, goal-centered answers.

Check in briefly with each group of two. Praise progress wherever you see it.

After each of the pairs seem to have reached a viable second draft, say, *Let's read the responses out loud and see what we have.*

Generate discussion about each individual's responses to the worksheet questions.

If someone chooses not to share his or her responses with the group, simply move on to the next person. Praise every person who reflects, in ways large or small, on possible strategies for bringing about a desired change in assignment. Where appropriate, add examples from your own personal experience.

Elicit suggestions from the group that seem relevant

to each person's situation. For example: "How could Tony get the credentials he needs?"

## VI. Activity: "Dealing With Organizational Stress"

The purpose of this group activity is to enable participants to uncover the most common controllable stress triggers they experience on a day- to-day basis.

Say: *Although there are many forms of stress we cannot predict or control (such as the trauma of being shot at) there are some stressors that are under our control. In this exercise, we will learn to do a better job of identifying and dealing with this kind of controllable stress. Part of what makes this such an interesting exercise is that each of us defines stress differently. What is stressful for you may not be stressful for me, and vice versa.*

Say: *Let me start by asking, what are some of the internal stressful aspects of this job?*

Write this sentence on a flip chart or display tool.

Say: *By "internal" I mean the stressful things that happen to us when we are on duty.*

Then go around the room and elicit a verbal response from each participant. As you actively listen to each person, help each speaker to clarify and articulate full responses. Very often, you will need to assist participants in developing very broad responses into more focused ones.

For example, you might hear someone state, "Supervisors" in response to this question. That's a good start, but you will want to initiate a little back and forth dialogue before you move on to the next person.

What exactly does this person mean when she says that supervisors are a stressful internal aspect of her job? Does she feel the supervisors are out of touch? Too demanding? Uninformed? Too hard on the cops who try to share problems with them? What is a specific example of how one or more supervisors have made her life more stressful? If it helps to move the conversation forward, you can encourage her to speak in general terms about the supervisors she has seen or heard about, rather than the one to whom she reports directly.

Remember, your job is to elicit comments from the group and help each member of the group take part in a dynamic discussion. That might mean asking others for feedback, or it might mean challenging, clarifying, probing, or refining someone's response.

After you have jotted down a few responses, you can begin to categorize them. The two categories you will use are: Organizational Stressful Events and Field-Related Stressful Events.

Following are examples for each category.

Organizational Stressful Events include:

- excessive paperwork ;
- unresponsive supervisors;
- inability to get time off;
- lack of promotional opportunities.

Field-Related Stressful Events include:

- overtime;
- nature of police work: exposure to "undesirable elements" in society;
- problems with partners.

As each person states what is stressful to him or her, the list will expand. Your job is to monitor the list, exclude any uncontrollable stressors (such as experiences of violence), and place the controllable stressors in the proper category.

Once you have a workable list, with sufficient entries in each category, say: *What we want to do now is explore the various ways we can manage and overcome the stressful events we have identified.*

Sometimes as officers, we fall victim to a certain way of looking at reality, and we may think we have less control over certain events than we actually do. We become trapped by unconscious ways of thinking. We experience things like criticism from supervisors, poor media coverage, and harassment from members of the public. We get used to building a negative world for ourselves, a world that sometimes leaves us to assume the worst about our experiences.

What I want us to do now is practice assuming the best. Practice looking past the negativity and the clouds. We're going to start that process by exploring new ways to handle some of the stressful situations we regularly experience.

Please break into groups of two and complete these worksheets.

Things That I Can Change About Myself to Better Cope with Organizational Stress

1. _____

2. _____

3. _____

4. _____

5. _____

Things That I Can Change About Myself to Better Cope with Field-Related Stress

1. _____

2. _____

3. _____

4. _____

5. _____

*Say*: *Once you are done, swap your work with your partner. After you have read what's there, offer your partner some of your own suggestions on how best to cope with specific stressors.*

*Revise your worksheet to incorporate the feedback you receive from your partner.*

Pair up with anyone who is left without a partner for this process. Help him or her to create constructive answers.

Check in briefly with each group of two. Praise progress wherever you see it.

After each of the pairs seems to have reached a viable second draft, say: *Let's read the responses out loud and see what we have.*

Generate discussion about each individual's responses to the worksheet questions.

If someone chooses not to share his or her responses with the group, simply move on to the next person. Praise every person who reflects, in ways large or small, on possible strategies for dealing with stress. Where appropriate, add examples from your own personal experience.

Elicit suggestions from the group that seem relevant to each person's situation. For example: "How could Mary address the problem she's describing with her supervisor?"

## VII. Activity: "Understanding And Managing Blind Rage"

The purpose of this group activity is to give participants a simulated experience of the kind of blind rage that officers may experience.

IMPORTANT: The exercise will not deliver good results unless you have established and reinforced a strong sense of group rapport. The participants trust each other (and you) to share the insights you will be asking them to provide.

Say: *Let me ask you a question: How would you define "blind rage"?*

Expect silence or requests for clarification the first time you pose this question.

Emphasize that you are looking for DEFINITIONS OF THE EXPERIENCE, not the "when" and "where" and "who" of what happened to anyone in particular.

Write down whatever answers the group provides by writing them on your flipchart or display tool, beneath the words BLIND RAGE.

Say: *A lot of officers have had this "blind rage" experience. Some of them describe it as "The moment I had tunnel vision." Does that ring any bells?*

Write: "The moment I had tunnel vision on your flip-chart or display tool.

Say: *Does anyone else have a different definition?*

Possible answers:

- "Losing it;"
- "Going off track."

Take down whatever answers the group provides by writing them on your flipchart or display tool, beneath the words BLIND RAGE.

Say: *That's great.*

Another definition you may hear for this experience is a little longer than the ones we've come up with here. It sounds like this: "The experience of a rage that is so singly focused and overwhelming that the person experiencing it cannot foresee the consequences of his or her behavior."

IMPORTANT: You must re-emphasize, probably several times, that you are not looking for "confessions" about when and where experiences of blind rage occurred. Once you have done that....

Your goal in posing this (difficult) question to is to get participants in touch with this experience.

Say: *Why should we talk about blind rage?*

Elicit responses from the members of the group.

Say: *Recognition often gives us a choice to do something about the experience – other than let it escalate.*

Say: *Now that we are clear that I am NOT asking you for the "wheres" and "whens" and "hows" of anyone's blind rage experience…*

*… let me ask you this ….*

*HOW DOES THE EXPERIENCE OF BLIND RAGE FEEL WHEN IT IS IN YOUR BODY?*

*For instance, some people describe their hands quivering.*

*HOW DID <u>YOU</u> SENSE IT? WHAT WERE THE SIGHTS, SOUNDS, FEELINGS, THOUGHTS, ETC.?*

Possible responses:

- Quivering in the hands or throughout the body
- Mind racing
- Feeling of heaviness in the eyes
- "Not seeing anything in front of me but the subject"
- Feeling overwhelmed
- "Having the single thought of teaching the subject a lesson"

Thank the participants for their honesty. Re-emphasize the point that identifying the details of the experience is to learn to be able to control it when it occurs.

Say: *What would happen if the person in a rage was not blind, but capable of seeing all there is to see in the situation?*

This question may confuse participants or result in a long silence. Be prepared to phrase it more than once, until the significance is understood. For instance, you may have to say: *We've called it blind rage … but how different could this experience be if we actually saw what was happening around us when we feel deep anger?*

The group may "get it" by nodding their heads, agreeing verbally, or suggesting their own strategies for maintaining the experience of being aware connection during an episode of rage.

Once you have seen evidence that the group "gets it" (and not before), continue by saying: *The nature of blind rage is such that we LOSE THE LARGER PERSPECTIVE.*

Wait for this to sink in, then continue by saying:

- We may lose perspective on our responsibilities to the department;

- We may lose perspective on our responsibilities to our families;

- We may lose perspective on our responsibilities to the people we serve;

- We may LOSE SIGHT of the impact of blind rage;

- *What if there was a way to experience anger where we didn't deny the emotion, but made a conscious effort to notice our surroundings?*

- *What if there was an OPEN-EYED RAGE?*

Discuss this possibility with the group. Elicit as many responses as you can and write them on the flipchart or display tool.

Once you have explored this possibility together, say: *An open-eyed or "seeing rage" tends to lower the intensity of the rage experience. The more we notice about our surroundings, the less likely we are to lose sight of our responsibilities.*

Encourage discussion of this idea. You should remain receptive throughout; you will certainly hear some interesting responses to this point.

Ask: *Now I want you to think of an IMAGINARY incident, something that happens in the future.*

*This is a MADE-UP incident that is capable of trigger-
ing what we ONCE experienced as "blind rage" ...*

*... but that we can choose to experience now as open-
eyed or seeing rage. What is that experience like? What do
you notice?*

Encourage each participant to share his or her fantasy experience of "open-eyed" rage with the group.

Expect many different variations on this fantasy
experience. You are looking for responses that indi-
cate the anger has lessened or subsided. Be sure to
praise and express thanks for any responses that show
this pattern.

Possible responses:

- "I don't feel as angry anymore."
- "I want to finish what I have to do and get out
  of there."
- "I want to talk the guy into calming down."

If a participant says that nothing really changes as a
result of this exercise, say: *Let's try this together* and ask
the question again as though it were directed solely at
him/her. If this still does not yield the desired outcome,

say: *There's another exercise we can do that may help.* (This refers to #6, "Outstanding Qualities," which you can do next.)

Share this quote:

> *No beating yourself up. That's not allowed! Be*
> *patient with yourself. It took you years to form*
> *the bad habits of thought that you no longer*
> *want. It will take a little time to form new*
> *and better ones. But I promise you this: even*
> *a slight move in this direction will bring you*
> *some peace. The more effort you apply to it, the*
> *faster you'll find your bliss, but you'll experience*
> *rewards immediately.*
> —HOLLY MOSIER

To bring closure to this exercise, ask: *What did you learn from this exercise?*

Do not be in too much of a hurry to bring the exercise to a close because the "closing question" you just asked may get some participants thinking about alternate responses to situations that trigger rage.

NOTE: It is extremely important that you take the

time to solicit opinions and encourage responses at this "What did you learn?" point in the discussion. It may be the most important part of the whole exercise. Once the group has examined the issues and personal discoveries in sufficient depth, you can conclude the exercise.

## VIII. Activity: "Understanding Qualities"

The purpose of this group activity is to get officers to identify their own outstanding attributes, particularly those that often get buried or go unacknowledged.

If you have just completed the "Managing Blind Rage" activity, say: *That is usually a very taxing exercise emotionally. I want to applaud you for completing it. It takes a lot of strength and courage to do that.*

Regardless of whether you have just completed the "Managing Blind Rage" activity, say: *Let's shift gears now and focus on one of my favorite topics: WHAT IS GREAT ABOUT YOU? After all, we need to be mindful about what works before we can get any real traction on what needs fixing. It's what you've got that works that will allow you to fix what needs fixing!*

*So let me ask you as a group: WHAT ARE SOME OF THE*

*OUTSTANDING QUALITIES OF POLICE OFFICERS?*

Emphasize that you are not asking individual officers to talk about their own strong suits, but the strong suits of police officers as a group.

Be prepared to "wait out" any pause or silence. If necessary, prompt the group by saying: *What are some of the positive qualities that make it possible for officers to do their job on a day-to-day basis?*

Write down whatever answers the group provides by writing them on your flipchart or display tool, beneath the words POSITIVE TRAITS.

Possible responses (with what you might write down shown in CAPITAL LETTERS:)

- Most officers get into law enforcement based on a desire to HELP OTHERS (discuss the specific examples);
- Most officers have a deeply GENEROUS SPIRIT and feel most fulfilled when they give of themselves (discuss the specific examples);
- Most officers end up making a POSITIVE DIFFERENCE in someone's life (discuss the specific examples);

- Most officers show great COURAGE; civilians run from a crisis, officers run toward it (discuss the specific examples);

- Most officers show great RESOURCEFUL-NESS, even in LIFE-THREATENING SITUATIONS. That's also called "grace under pressure"—you could also call it "experience" (discuss the specific examples);

- Most officers work under extremely DIFFICULT CONDITIONS (Discuss the specific examples. If necessary, prompt with: dark side of human nature, bad weather, dangerous situations without preparation, separation from family time);

- Most officers have great PERSEVERANCE. You actually can't do the job well without it. Not everybody is cut out to address potential crisis, day after day (discuss the specific examples).

Ask: *Why do you think it is so common for most of these qualities to be overlooked or minimized—even by officers?*

Record the group's responses on your flipchart or display tool.

Possible responses:

- Internal routine; officers, themselves, come to take these qualities for granted;
- Media shorthand; negative qualities often more interesting than positive ones;
- Public comes to expect certain things (not surprised when it happens).

To bring closure to this exercise, ask: *What did you learn from this exercise?*

Do not be in too much of a hurry to bring the exercise to a close because the "closing question" you just asked may get some participants thinking about their own positive qualities and why they are often ignored by others.

## IX. Activity: "LETTING GO OF CYNICISM"

The purpose of this group activity is to show officers what cynicism is and how it becomes a habit in day-to-day life.

Say: *Let me ask you a question: WHAT IS CYNICISM? What does that word mean to you?*

Write down the responses on the flipchart or display tool.

Responses may include:

- Not caring as much as you once did;
- Giving up;
- Just going through the motions;
- Being negative about things;


Say: *Those are all good answers. Here's how the diction-ary defines CYNICISM.*

Write or reveal this definition on your flipchart or display tool: *"An expression of distrust born out of a belief that human conduct is motivated mostly by self-interest."*

Say: *Who wants to try to translate that into everyday English for me?*

Be prepared to "wait out" any pause or silence. If necessary, prompt the group by saying: *How is someone who is CYNICAL likely to feel about taking risks for other people?* Discuss this point with the group until you reach a practical definition like the following: "Everybody is looking out for #1; no one really cares about me."

Say: *What are some behaviors officers may engage in when they feel cynical?* Examples will vary widely depending on the group. Write down the responses you receive on the flipchart or display tool.

Say: *Most of us have acted in ways like this when we are*

*feeling cynical. I know I certainly have. Is cynical behavior a plus or a minus for us when we engage in it?* Examples will vary widely depending on the group. Create two columns: PLUS and MINUS.

Write down the responses you receive on the flip-chart or display tool under the proper column. Discuss the results.

Say: *Let me ask you another question. How do you think cynical actions and beliefs can affect our "off-duty" life?*

Write down the responses you receive on the flip-chart or display tool. Discuss the responses.

Say: *As a general rule, cynical attitudes, beliefs and actions are based on disappointing experiences we have had in the past. I'm talking about times when we did not feel appreciated, acknowledged, or valued. The feelings we have from those experiences can get carried into the future.*

Ask: *What kinds of experiences are likely to make officers feel like that?*

Possible responses include:

- Family disapproval of long hours
- Hostility from civilians
- Problems with supervisors

Encourage the participants to offer detail on the examples they share. When the examples have been discussed fully, say: *I've got something I'd like to read to you.*

*It is important to realize that while cynicism is a natural response that arises from being taken for granted, from feeling unappreciated and unvalued, it is also a response that minimizes us and creates an even greater sense of powerlessness. Cynicism defeats us before we even begin to respond to any aspect of police work. Whenever the mind is zapped with cynicism, it cannot use its energy to be optimistic, to trust others, or to turn negative situations into positive ones. In time, even relationships between members of the force suffer; this is in addition, of course, to all the other negative consequences listed above. We must break the cycle of cynicism for our own good, and the good of the people who depend on us. If we don't break that cycle, cynicism can damage our relationships and our own sense of well-being irreparably.*

—Dr. Deborah Moore

Say: *Do you agree or disagree?*

Discuss the responses.

Say: *Cynicism about our relationships with others is the opposite of being optimistic about those relationships. Cynicism means assuming there will be problems and no one will care about whether they are solved. Unfortunately, this is often a self-fulfilling prophecy.*

To close out this exercise, ask: *What are some of the ways we can build up optimism in our relationships with others, both on and off duty?*

Discuss the results and record them on the flipchart or on your display tool.

# X. Activity: "STRESS MANAGEMENT"

## COMMON RESPONSES TO STRESS

### Physiological Responses

- Vague physical complaints
- Sweaty palms
- Dilated pupils
- Trembling
- Bodily responses such as stomach ailments and digestion problems
- Headaches/backaches
- Significant weight gain or loss
- Lack of sleep
- Too much sleep
- Chronic fatigue

### Emotions

- Apparently disproportionate sadness
- Lack of focus
- Daydreaming
- Frequent mood changes
- Apparently disproportionate anger
- Memory lapses
- Irritability
- Anger

### Behaviors

- Explosive outbursts
- Constant complaining
- Increased dependence on alcohol or other substances
- Diminished attention to detail
- Cynical or hostile remarks
- Overly critical of others
- Insubordinate to supervisors
- Downward changes in job productivity
- Withdrawn (when this was not part of behavior before stress)
- Increased self-criticism
- Generally negative disposition
- Impulsive actions

Distribute the Common Responses To Stress chart.

Say: *Although almost everybody at one time or another has experienced stress, the way it is experienced differs sharply, depending on the individual. That means it's important that we look at how individual officers respond to stress … and what our own personal responses are.* While discussing this chart, ask members to identify how fellow officers, and they, themselves, are likely to react to stress in the work environment. Ask what elements they would add to each category on the chart. Record the responses on your flipchart or display tool.

Share your own experiences in discovering your own responses to stress.

When each person can discuss his or her own response to stressful events, and the responses of others in his or her world, distribute the Stress Identification Profile and ask each participant to complete it individually. Discuss the results to the degree that your group is comfortable doing so, then conclude this exercise.

## Stress Identification Profile (SIP)

Use this Stress Identification Profile to identify your personal reactions to stress.

Although an individual's reaction to stressful situations differs from person to person, most of us are able to recognize certain distinctive personal characteristics when we are under stress. Moreover, a person's coping skills will also differ. Some people display stronger initial coping styles than others do. For many people, identifying an effective stress management response takes time and practice. Recognizing this fact is a victory, not a defeat.

Identifying how your body and mind responds to stress is essential if you want to control your behavior. One of the reasons officers experience being "out of control" in ways large and small is *they are not aware they are experiencing stress in the first place.* It is important to learn to recognize the indicators of stress, which are expressed uniquely in each individual, in order to prepare yourself to deal with stress.

**When it comes to stress management, a proactive stance is always healthier than a reactive stance. Take control of the situation before it takes control of you!**

Your first objective is simple: identify your current reactions. A list of common responses appears at the bottom of this page. Use that list for reference when filling out this sheet. Which responses and coping strategies seem most authentic to your own personal experience?

Your second objective is also simple: identify your current coping strategies. When you know you must compose yourself in response to a stressful situation, and you do so successfully, what concrete actions do you take? Do you take a long deep breath? Do you remove yourself from the situation for a few moments? Do you say a certain phrase to yourself silently? Do you ask for help from a higher power? Do you create a mental picture you can focus on, a picture that helps you re-establish a purposeful sense of self?

## Physiological Responses

1. _____

2. _____

3. _____

4. _____

5. _____

6. _____


## Emotional Responses

1. _____

2. _____

3. _____

4. _____

5. _____

6. _____


## Behavioral Responses

1. _____

2. _____

3. _____

4. _____

5. _____

6. _____


## How I cope with stress

1. _____

2. _____

3. _____

4. _____

5. _____

6. _____

## Common Responses to Stress

### PHYSIOLOGICAL

- racing or pounding heart
- excessive perspiration
- cold sweaty palms
- rapid breathing
- asthma attack
- constipation
- high blood pressure
- dry mouth
- headaches
- tics or twitching muscles
- change in appetite
- impaired sexual function
- weight change
- itching
- skin rash
- colds or the flu

### EMOTIONAL

- difficulty concentrating
- forgetfulness
- feelings of being sad
- suspiciousness
- racing thoughts
- feelings of anxiety
  or panic
- mood swings
- excessive anger
- inability to enjoy things
  you used to enjoy
- apathy
- cynicism
- withdrawn socially
  and psychologically
- changed interest in sex
- restlessness

### BEHAVIORAL

- erratic work habits
- excessive worrying
- increased use of sick time
- over/under eating
- change in sleep patterns
- angry outbursts
- nightmares
- increased craving
  for sweets
- gritting teeth
- nail biting
- constant crying
- excessive complaints

# EPILOGUE

# *The Master Class*

**B**efore we conclude, let me share some good advice on stress management—and life management—from some people I would consider master counselors. Regard this section of the book your master class in helping yourself, so you can do a better job of helping others.

> *You'll get mixed up, of course, as you already*
> *know. You'll get mixed up with many strange*
> *birds as you go. So be sure when you step. Step*
> *with care and great tact and remember that*
> *Life's a Great Balancing Act. Just never forget*

*to be dexterous and deft. And never mix up your*
*right foot with your left.*
—Dr. Seuss, *Oh, the Places You'll Go!* (2003)


*Holding onto anger is like holding onto a*
*hot coal with the intention of throwing it at*
*someone. You are the one who is burned.*
—The Buddha


*HELPED are those who risk themselves for*
*others' sakes; to them will be given increasing*
*opportunities for ever greater risks. Theirs will*
*be a vision of the world in which no one's gift*
*is despised or lost.*

*HELPED are those who strive to give up*
*their anger; their reward will be that in any*
*confrontation their first thoughts will never be*
*of violence or of war.*

*HELPED are those whose every act is a*
*prayer for peace; on them depends the future of*
*the world.*

*HELPED are those who forgive; their reward*
*shall be forgiveness of every evil done to them.*

*It will be in their power, therefore, to envision*
*the new Earth.*
*HELPED are those who are shown the*
*existence of the Creator's magic in the*
*Universe; they shall experience delight and*
*astonishment without ceasing.*
*HELPED are those who laugh with a pure*
*heart; theirs will be the company of the*
*jolly righteous.*
—ALICE WALKER

*These are the things I learned (in Kindergarten):*
1. *Share everything.*
2. *Play fair.*
3. *Don't hit people.*
4. *Put things back where you found them.*
5. *CLEAN UP YOUR OWN MESS.*
6. *Don't take things that aren't yours.*
7. *Say you're SORRY when you*
   *HURT somebody.*
8. *Wash your hands before you eat.*
9. *Flush.*
10. *Warm cookies and cold milk are good for you.*

11. *Live a balanced life—learn some and drink some and draw some and paint some and sing and dance and play and work everyday some.*

12. *Take a nap every afternoon.*

13. *When you go out into the world, watch out for traffic, hold hands, and stick together.*

14. *Be aware of wonder. Remember the little seed in the Styrofoam cup: The roots go down and the plant goes up and nobody really knows how or why, but we are all like that.*

15. *Goldfish and hamster and white mice and even the little seed in the Styrofoam cup— they all die. So do we.*

16. *And then remember the Dick-and-Jane books and the first word you learned—the biggest word of all—LOOK."*

   —ROBERT FULGHUM, *All I Really Need to Know I Learned in Kindergarten* (2004)


*He knows that you have to laugh at the things that hurt you just to keep yourself in balance, just to keep the world from running you plumb crazy.*
—KEN KESEY, *One Flew Over the Cuckoo's Nest* (1962)

*Excellence is never an accident. It is always*
*the result of high intention, sincere effort, and*
*intelligent execution; it represents the wise*
*choice of many alternatives—choice, not chance,*
*determines your destiny.*
—ARISTOTLE

*Even a happy life cannot be without a measure*
*of darkness, and the word happy would lose its*
*meaning if it were not balanced by sadness.*
—C.G. JUNG

And one more. James A, Michener once wrote: "The master in the art of living makes little distinction between his work and his play, his labor and his leisure, his mind and his body, his information and his recreation, his love and his religion. He hardly knows which is which. He simply pursues his vision of excellence at whatever he does, leaving others to decide whether he is working or playing. To him he's always doing both." It's been my aim here to make it easy for you to create a life as a law enforcement officer that is so deeply committed to excellence, so well balanced, and so closely harmonized with the mission of your department and your family, that you are always doing what you love. May we all become such masters of living.

Please continue the journey towards life mastery by visiting me at www.drdebimoore.org —and tell me about your experiences using the tactics I've shared in this book.

# *References*

Adams, Douglass. 2002. *The Salmon of Doubt.* New York: Random House.

Dictionary.com. Accessed September 8, 2012, http://dictionary.reference.com

Dr. Suess. 2003. *Oh the Places You'll Go.* London: Harper Collins.

Fulghum, Robert. 2004. *All I Really Need to Know I Learned in Kindergarten.* New York: Random House.

"How Common Are Panic Attacks?" The Health Centre. Accessed August 5, 2012, http://www.thehealthcenter.info/adult-panic-attacks/how-common-are-panic-attacks.htm.

Kesey, Ken. 1962. *One Flew Over the Cuckoo's Nest.* New York: Viking Press.

Moore, Deborah C. "The Impact of Occupational Stress and the Effectiveness of Stress Coping Strategies on Marital Relationships of Police Officers." Diss., Capella University, 2004.

O'Hara, Andrew, and John Violanti. "Police Suicide: A Comprehensive Study of 2008 National Data." *Journal of Emergency Mental Health.* (November 2009) 11 (1): 17-23.

Ralifson, F. M., and P. J. Heaton. 1995. "Police Problems identified." *Law & Order, 13.*

Rowling, J.K. 2007 *Harry Potter and the Deathly Hallows.* New York: Scholastic Inc.

"The National Survey of Sexual Health and Behavior." Centre for Sexual Health Promotion. Last modified October, 2010, http://www.nationalsexstudy. indiana.edu.

United States Army. 1983. *Army Leadership: Eleven Principles of Army Leadership.* U.S. Government Printing Office: Washington DC.

Violanti, John. 2007. *Police Suicide: Epidemic in Blue.* Springfield, Illinois: Charles C Thomas Publisher.

# PART III

*Appendices*

# APPENDIX I

# *On-Line Resources*

I've come up with a set of rules that describe our reactions to technologies:

1. *Anything that is in the world when you're born is normal and ordinary and is just a natural part of the way the world works.*
2. *Anything that's invented between when you're fifteen and thirty-five is new and exciting and revolutionary and you can probably get a career in it.*
3. *Anything invented after you're thirty-five is against the natural order of things.*

—Douglas Adams, *The Salmon of Doubt* (2002)

We are blessed to live in a connected age, an age where our technology and our communication tools give us access to a wider array of resources than past generations of law enforcement professionals. There are a number of great on-line resources for police officers who want to leverage the Internet and social media as tools for effective stress management and life management. Below are some of my favorites.

### Human Development Services:
### WWW.DRDEBIMOORE.ORG

Of course, I invite you to visit my site first. There, you will learn to:

- Implement proven stress management techniques designed specifically for law enforcement professionals

- Change the way you think and behave, through the E.B.C. Method

- Let go of anger and other unwanted feelings

- Recognize the ways in which you are not living a fully authentic life

- Develop meaningful relationships

- Improve your communication skills
- Manage conflict more effectively
- Improve focus & productivity
- Jump start your goals
- Live a happier & healthier life

## WWW.COPSALIVE.COM

An excellent blog devoted to "saving the lives of the people who save lives."

## WWW.POLICEONE.COM

Provides relevant topics about the law enforcement community.

## WWW.TEARSOFACOP.COM

Support-themed website for officers dealing with stress, PTSD, family counseling, and related issues.

## 101+ STRESS MANAGEMENT TECHNIQUES FOR POLICE OFFICERS

A big, visually compelling poster that deserves to hang in every precinct in the country. Check it out at: http://stresshealthsolutions.com/wordpress/?p=89

## WWW.POLICEPTSD.COM

Web site for the on-line community devoted to supporting those who have experienced police-related traumatic stress. The site states: "Regardless of your occupation or your critical incident, PolicePTSD.com and its members can help. Register anonymously with just a first name."

## WWW.POLICEMENTALHEALTH.BLOGSPOT.COM

Excellent blog addressing mental health and family therapy issues of interest to law enforcement professionals.

## WWW.POLICESTRESSDOC.COM

An innovative environment for law enforcement officers to share, exchange, and connect with other officers about various topics ranging from patrol experiences to family issues.

## POLICE FAMILY LIFE

An active discussion board for spouses, children, parents, or siblings of law enforcement officers. Check it out at: http://policelink.monster.com/discussions/120-police-family-life/topics

# WWW.WOMENANDPOLICING.COM

The website for the National Center for Women & Policing (NCWP), which "promotes increasing the numbers of women at all ranks of law enforcement as a strategy to improve police response to violence against women, reduce police brutality and excessive force, and strengthen community policing reforms."

## POLICE FAMILY VIOLENCE FACT SHEET

An important overview of a critical law enforcement challenge from the National Center for Women and Policing. Check it out at: http://womenandpolicing.com/violenceFS.asp

## NATIONAL BLACK POLICE ASSOCIATION

The nationwide organization of African American Police Associations "dedicated to the promotion of justice, fairness, and effectiveness in law enforcement." The NBPA has several chartered organizations throughout the United States. It serves as an advocate for minority police officers and establishes a national network for the training and education of police officers and others interested in law enforcement. Check out the organization's web site at www.blackpolice.com.

## WWW.GOALNY.ORG

The web site for Goal-NY, the Gay Officers Action League, "serving LGBT Criminal Justice Professionals. Law Enforcement Officers from all agencies." According to the web site, "friends are welcome to join."

# About
# Dr. Deborah C. Moore

Deborah C. Moore, Ph.D., LMFT is a licensed Marriage and Family Therapist and a retired Lieutenant in the New York City Police Department. She is the founder of Human Development Services, which specializes in stress management and leadership development. These services empower individuals and organizations to manage stressful life events, reach their maximum potential, and achieve important life goals.

Dr. Moore offers the following resources:

- PERSONAL COACHING: Coaching services offer individuals an opportunity to work on a specific area of development in a practical manner with solution-focused results.
- CONFLICT RESOLUTION: Learn ways to mitigate conflict and develop healthy relationships with others.

- BUSINESS COACHING: Learn techniques to create a successful business and superb team leadership skills.

Dr. Moore is available to speak on the following topics:

- Stress Management 101
- Anger Management
- Crisis Intervention/ Critical Incident Stress Management
- Conflict Resolution
- Domestic Violence Awareness Training
- Motivation & Success
- Dealing with Difficult Supervisors
- Dealing with Difficult Employees
- Dealing with Difficult Co-workers
- Dating and the Busy Professional

*For more information on Dr. Moore and her work, visit www.drdebimoore.org.*

CPSIA information can be obtained at www.ICGtesting.com
Printed in the USA
LVOW011540030413

327447LV00018B/778/P